Land *of the* Porcupine

Growing up in Madawaska

Land *of the* Porcupine

Growing up in Madawaska

By Ronald Stewart

SALT PONDS PRESS
A division of Islandport Press

YARMOUTH • FRENCHBORO • MAINE

Maine books from Islandport Press
www.islandportpress.com

The Cows Are Out!
by Trudy Chambers Price

A Moose and a Lobster Walk into a Bar
by John McDonald

Silas Crockett
by Mary Ellen Chase

Here for Generations: The Story of a Maine Bank and its City
by Dean Lawrence Lunt

In Maine
by John N. Cole

The Story of Mount Desert Island
by Samuel Eliot Morison

A History of Little Cranberry Island
by Hugh L. Dwelley

Hauling by Hand: The Life and Times of a Maine Island
by Dean Lawrence Lunt

Children's Books

When I'm With You
by Elizabeth Elder; illustrated by Leslie Mansmann

Please visit www.islandportpress.com for more information about all the great books available from Islandport Press.

Reading Groups

Reading Group materials are available for some Islandport Press books. For more information, visit www.islandportpress.com or call 207-846-4563.

Salt Ponds Press
P.O. Box 10
Yarmouth, Maine 04096
saltponds@islandportpress.com
www.islandportpress.com

ISBN: 0-9763231-0-9
Library of Congress Control Number: 2004098912

First Edition Published November 2004

Book design by Salt Ponds Press
Cover design by Karen F. Hoots / Mad Hooter Design
Cover photo of Ronald Stewart courtesy of Ronald Stewart
Interior photos courtesy of Ronald Stewart

Dedication

I dedicate my first book to my wife, Shirley, with much love and appreciation for her assistance throughout this endeavor.

Acknowledgments

I acknowledge so many for the wonderful life I have enjoyed over the years.

The inhabitants of the St. John Valley, from whom I learned the meaning of family, love and the importance of joie de vivre.

My hunting friends, from whom I learned the importance and beauty of the Maine woods.

My golfing friends, from whom I learned that it's not the winning that's important, but the camaraderie.

And most of all, my four children, Judith, Gordon, Nancy and Douglas, who have made me proud of their respective successes in their own lives and who have encouraged me to finish this memoir.

God bless Shirley, my wife of fifty-four years, for everything she has done for me, and for helping me with the completion of this book.

And my mother and father, who made me proud to be their son, and who are waiting for me in heaven, if God lets me in to see them again.

Contents

	Foreword	xiii
1	Scottish Influence	1
2	Preschool Memories	7
3	My First Real Home	13
4	Skating, Skiing, Sliding	17
5	Radio Entertainment	21
6	First Year of School, Mud Season	25
7	Summer Activities	33
8	Family Reunions	39
9	Nighthawks, Bats and Death	51
10	Potatoes, Hunting and Halloween	55
11	Family Guidance and Father's Moods	65
12	My Mother, the Family Peacemaker	75
13	French Family Influence	81
14	Madawaska Pay Nights	85
15	Teenager, 1938	89
16	Humor Offsets World Concerns	93
17	Facing Discrimination	99
18	Working in the Mill	103
19	College and Navy Enlistment	107
20	Adjusting to Civilian Life	115
21	*G-8 and His Battle Aces*	119
22	Married Life	125
23	Our First Child, Judith Denise	135
24	Roger Berube, First Selectman	139
25	Good Times Remembered	147
26	Father Cyr and Father Menard	151
27	The Land of the Porcupine	155
	Epilogue	159
	About the Author	161

Foreword

As I grow older and wonder how many years I have left to enjoy the beauty of this earth and to reflect upon the passage of times that I have enjoyed, I realize that my own children have reached an age that I once thought old—some of their children are teenagers and beyond.

So many times have I wished that I had been more quizzical of my own parents' younger days and asked about their relationships, feelings about life, thoughts, joys, and times of sadness. I am now seventy-nine years of age and do not profess to be a man of letters, but I do have memories that I wish to share with my family, friends, and any other readers who have a few moments to spend with me.

Whenever someone asks me about my origins, I always answer that my hometown is Madawaska. In most instances the next question will be, "Where in hell is that?" (This question always triggers in my mind a Portland television advertisement that repeatedly stated, "You can't get there from here.") I am always polite, and explain that Madawaska is located in the St. John Valley in northern Maine.

Geographically, Madawaska is the most northern town in Maine (even though Fort Kent often claims this distinction). It is some 400-plus miles north of Kittery, Maine, and is separated from the province of New Brunswick, Canada, and the city of Edmundston by the St. John River, which provides a boundary between the United States and Canada, and which was established by the Webster-Ashburton Treaty in 1842.

Madawaska, translated from the Maliseet Indian language, means the "Land of the Porcupine." I have often wondered why the area was so named, since never in my twenty-eight years of residency there did I ever cross paths with a porcupine.

My greatest memories in life came from my younger years in the town I have always considered my home. The town provided me with lasting friendships, peaceful times, many laughs, few sorrows, a closeness to nature, and a feeling of equality with those I knew. My life today continues to be a happy one, filled with memories of past adventures in the Land of the Porcupine. It is of this time that I reflect upon in my memories of the past.

Ronald Stewart
Bath, Maine
September 2004

Chapter One

Scottish Influence

I was born of Scottish blood, and from the time before I was born, the Scots have influenced where I lived and what has become of me in later years.

My father and my mother were born in Canada, as I was. My father was a farm boy who left his family farm and enlisted in the Canadian Army in 1915. He spent the next three years in France as part of a Canadian force that fought the Germans in World War I. While on liberty in Saint John, New Brunswick, before he left for England, he met my mother, an Irish lass by the name of Mary Conway. Mary was impressed by the good-looking young man, Gordon H. Stewart, and she wrote him often while he was overseas and greeted him when he returned to New Brunswick in 1919.

Their new romance was interrupted by my father's employment with the Canadian National Railroad as a cook for a work crew in McAdam Junction in New Brunswick. Missing Mary very much, he returned to Saint John and asked her to marry him. She didn't hesitate to say "yes," and they were married in 1920.

With a wife to support, my father accepted a job offer with a lumber company in Estcourt, Quebec. The new mill was constructed to process logs being cut along the St. Francis River and its tributaries. The lumber company was one of many expansion plans of Fraser Paper Company Limited. At the time, my father didn't realize he would soon participate in another phase of Fraser's growth, one that would take him to the United States and interrupt the idyllic life he and my mother enjoyed in the woods of Quebec, where they lived in a small bungalow in view of Pohenegamook Lake, which bordered the town.

Several times in later life when I was old enough to travel, and we had our first automobile, we returned to Estcourt to see their former home. We visited sites familiar to them, and I would pick up on stories they told of their early years of marriage. Living in Estcourt was the happiest of times for both. They told me about their lumbering experiences and snowshoeing through the woods with friends, and about how they appreciated visits from relatives who took the adventurous trip by train to spend time with them.

My father, according to my mother, was overjoyed to see the relatives, but in her words, he always "acted the fool" to entertain everyone. This was a trait of my father's that carried throughout his life, and which provided many jovial moments.

As a newly married couple, my parents spent much of their free time playing tennis, which seemed to me to be such an unlikely sport for a frontier village like Estcourt. But the Frasers (the mill owners) were lovers of tennis, and so tennis courts were built for their enjoyment. They thought well enough of their employees and other townspeople to share the courts with them, and often arranged for weekend matches.

As a result of my father's decision to leave the province of New Brunswick for the province of Quebec, my life was greatly impacted by another man of Scottish birth—the founder of Fraser Paper.

Long before my father's birth, a Scot by the name of Donald Fraser of Aberdeen decided to leave Scotland in April of 1873 with some 600 Scottish men, women and children, boarding the steamship *Castelia* at Glasgow, and sailing for Canada where they planned to form a colony in Kincardine in New Brunswick. Donald, age thirty-one, was accompanied by his wife and two young sons, Archibald and Donald Jr. They arrived in Saint John, New Brunswick, on May 10, 1873, to begin life in a country that only six years earlier had become the Dominion of Canada.

They traveled up the St. John River by boat to Kilburn and walked into Kincardine where they established their colony. They cleared and cultivated the land, while others worked on the railroad that was being constructed northward along the St. John River. Donald Fraser cleared his 200-acre lot for his home and shortly after took steps to establish his livelihood from lumbering.

In 1873, Donald purchased a small sawmill, and his venture flourished. As his sons grew into young men, they joined their father, and in 1892, they became partners with him in the firm of Donald Fraser and Sons. In 1895, the new company built a large sawmill in Fredericton, New Brunswick.

Later, fellow immigrants to Kincardine teamed up with Donald and his sons. The new group expanded their lumber business, and by 1916, the company was the largest of its kind in the Maritime Provinces of Canada, if not the largest in Eastern Canada. In 1915, a sawmill was built in Estcourt, Quebec. This particular addition to the Fraser holdings played a significant role in my father's life and mine. Donald Fraser died in 1916. At the time of his death, he was operating nine sawmills in the provinces of Quebec and New Brunswick.

Although my parents hoped for an early family, my mother had problems conceiving; five years had passed after the year of their marriage before my mother excitedly told my father that a child was on the way. There were no doctors in Estcourt, and little assistance for my mother to give birth to her first child. She decided that she would have her baby in the farmhouse in which my father had been born and raised. She traveled alone from Estcourt to St. George, New Brunswick, on the Canadian National Railroad, which connected with several subsidiary lines in the CNR system. She was met by her husband's father, Wallace Stewart, and was driven by horse and buggy to his home on the Manor Road. It was a simple and homey white clapboard farmhouse on the shores of the Magaguadavic River, a Maliseet word meaning "River of Eels."

She spent her time writing letters to her loved one, and he wrote to her, as both anxiously waited for the birth, which occurred on June 8, 1925, when Ronald Edward Wallace Stewart came into the world.

Later in life, I grew to dislike my name and the fact that I had been provided with two middle names—Edward, after my mother's father, Edward Conway, and Wallace, after my other grandfather. Assuming my mother had named me, I blamed her.

It wasn't until 1983, after my mother had passed away, that I learned she had not given me the name Ronald. I was sorting out her belongings and came across a letter that my father had written to her in 1925, which she had saved for fifty-eight years. In the letter written a week or so before I was born, he had written, "If you have a son, I would like you to name him Ronald. If you have a daughter, I don't give a damn what you name her." Knowing my father as I learned to over the years, he would have loved a daughter just as much as he had loved me.

The year of my birth marked another milestone in the expansion effort of Fraser Paper, which later became its corporate name. In 1925, a two-machine paper mill was built in Madawaska, Maine, to complement a 120-ton per day pulp mill on the Canadian side of the St. John River in Edmundston. The manufactured pulp was pumped in liquid form across the International Bridge spanning the St. John River to the Madawaska mill. The pipeline across the bridge had an additional value to the company's profits, in that pulp shipped to the United States in liquid form escaped the payment of duties imposed on the importation of dry pulp. Who says the Scots aren't ingenious?

My father, having worked for the Fraser family for three years before the paper mill opened in Madawaska, and being known as a responsible employee, was offered a position as foreman of the beater room at the new paper mill. He gratefully accepted, and we moved to Edmundston in the fall of 1925. My father commuted into Maine for work each day until the following spring, when on April 10, 1926, we crossed the International Bridge to live in Madawaska. Our new home was one of the new company houses in the area of what would later be named Mill Street.

And so begins my story of growing up in the Land of the Porcupine.

CHAPTER TWO

Preschool Memories

The St. John Valley is located in both Canada and the United States and is separated by the St. John River. The river was established as the boundary between the two countries as a result of the Webster-Ashburton Treaty in 1842, which settled the dispute with Great Britain over the boundary between Maine and Canada.

Eight centuries earlier, an Indian tribe of the Algonquin family had arrived. Their descendants, now known as the Maliseets, still call the area *Madawaskaki*, translated to mean, "Land of the Porcupine."

The Maliseet tribe subsisted mainly from animal products, fashioning warm clothing and moccasins from the skins. From the bones, they whittled tools and utensils. From the sinew, they fashioned strips of leather. The men built canoes, and the women wove baskets, tanned hides and laced snowshoes. They enjoyed an isolated existence.

In the summer of 1785, a group of canoes carrying bedraggled French Acadian families arrived. The families had been driven out of Nova Scotia by the British, who chased them up the St. John River. However, an area that is now known as Grand Falls, New Brunswick, limited the pursuit. The falls prevented the British vessels from traveling any further north.

The Acadians took refuge in what was to become the American side of the river at an area now known as St. David, a parish now part of Madawaska. The Acadians were the first white men to be greeted by the Maliseets of the Upper St. John Valley. Desperate to find a home away from British tyranny, the Acadians were grateful for their Indian friends' warm welcome.

Throughout the 1800s, the timber-rich region lured many other families from other parts of the Maritime Provinces and Upper Canada. As a result, a mixture of ethnic groups mingled peacefully. Irish, Scottish, American, French Canadians and English pioneers, lured by dreams of wealth and independence, came together. Sawmills expanded, the railroads arrived, pulp mills and paper mills became economically important, and commerce stimulated the economy. Houses were being built and stores, including Gardner's Store and Rice's Furniture, were arriving on Main Street. Side streets remained dirt roads, though, and municipal facilities were limited to the construction of water lines.

I have no memories whatsoever of living in Edmundston, New Brunswick, a small city of about 25,000 people, on the Canadian side of the International Bridge. My first memory of Madawaska, at around age four, was about my father. He had just bought his first automobile. It was a bright blue Pontiac sedan, and it gave him a feeling of self-importance. I recall that we were parked at the top of Bridge Street (as it was then named) next to the dirt sidewalk, my father sitting with the front window lowered and a wide grin on his face as the mill workers walked by. They would stop to chat and make complimentary remarks about his 1929 Pontiac. My Dad was on cloud nine.

From that time on, he took pride in his automobiles and traded every second year.

Memories of happenings before I entered school are difficult to recall, but my mother always told me how another playmate and I, at about the age of three, ate all the leaves of one of her houseplants. I only recall hiding behind the living room couch so we wouldn't be caught for something, so we must have been guilty of what she later told me.

Most of my preschool memories relate to snow, for snow became our favorite toy. We could mold it, throw it, eat it, freeze it, pile it, carve it, and melt it. Snow provided almost never-ending entertainment. From the start, I was a "winter person," loving the coolness of the frosty air and the beauty of oversized snowflakes slowly falling from the sky and covering the landscape with a white blanket of new enjoyment. Winter was always more enjoyable to me than the hot, sticky discomfort of summer.

Building snow caves provokes my strongest recollections of fun in the snow. During my early school years I spent many hours shoveling and digging out the caves in the hours after school and before my eight o'clock curfew. Winter storms seemed more severe in the 1920s and early '30s, but this may have been caused by my newness to the world, and my relative size to the environment. I have visited some of the old play areas that I thought were so huge as a child, only to find that they were nothing more than postage stamp–sized lots.

Picard's Field, named after its owner, Abel Picard, was our principal playground, and although it has been fully developed

Main Street in Madawaska, probably in the 1940s.

today, it was a fair-sized play area for neighborhood children back then. The snow would drift beyond the slopes of the field, creating hardened banks of snow that could easily be shaped with shovels carried from home. We would trudge across the field, through waist-high snow, dragging our shovels behind us, and upon reaching the wind-packed drifts, begin scooping out shovelful after shovelful until we had completed a maze of connecting caves. Our imaginations fostered a belief that our caves stretched for miles. I suspect that our caves never really stretched beyond forty feet.

At various intervals throughout our system of caves, a hatch—a hole covered with a piece of cardboard—was placed that allowed us to escape upward should it be necessary to do so, although I can't believe we ever worried about the weight of the snow collapsing or the possibility of suffocation. The real purpose of the hatch was to allow light into some of the darker areas of the caves. As I think about this today, it is surprising that our parents weren't more concerned about possible cave-ins, as the drifts in some areas were six and seven feet high, and we would construct the caves as close to ground level as possible. For the late afternoons we brought candles to light our way, setting them on "mantles" that we carved along the inside walls of the passageways. When the air seemed smoky, or when we sensed a lightness in the air quality, we would open one of the escape hatches and allow the cold, frigid air to sweep through our world beneath the snow.

In the center of our maze, we constructed an oversized area that served as a meeting chamber where we huddled our small bodies together and told stories. Our thoughts often turned to fantasies of the world around us. We talked about the stars and the moon and wondered about life and ourselves, although we were very naive about everything in general.

Picard's Field was all that we needed to enjoy winter. The same cave-riddled slopes, hardened by the winter winds, were also used for ski jumps. We would pile snow halfway down a slope, pack it down firmly with a shovel, and move a ski back and forth across it to create a track. Then we were ready to soar off into space. Again, I feel certain that we never jumped more than five or six feet at the most, but our fantasies allowed us to imagine that we were equal to some of the long-distance jumpers of that era, and that jumping records were being broken daily in Picard's Field!

If we didn't care to jump, we could always just ski. There were no ski lifts in Picard's Field, nor did any of us have ski boots. We did have makeshift bindings on our skis. If we were lucky enough to find a discarded inner tube from an automobile tire, it was cut into one-inch strips. This self-created rubberband would be pulled over our gum-rubbers, or winter boots. With our foot placed firmly in the leather strap of the ski, the inner tube "binding" would be stretched from the back of the boot over the toe of the boot after passing through the ski's leather strap. Somehow, this binding held the boot on the ski, except when the plate of the ski would build up with compacted snow or ice. Then the boot would slide off the ski, making a successful run down the hill very difficult.

No one seemed to mind if the ski came off and raced down the hill without the skier. We would simply retrieve the ski and trudge back up the hill for another try. It wasn't as easy as one might imagine, however, as the snow was deep, and the skis were very cumbersome to handle because of their size. They were made of wood, usually five or more inches in width, and two to four times our height in length. They were extremely heavy and not easy to maneuver. We didn't do "snowplows" or "christies." We skied straight downhill, or in whichever direction the skis were pointed when we started, and we stopped when the length of our ski trail ended. If it was necessary to stop before that time, we fell, and often plowed through snow that covered our bodies.

It was next to impossible to sidestep or herringbone our way back up to the summit of the hill because of the awkwardness of the skis, so whether we had made a successful run down the hill, or were retrieving a runaway ski, it was necessary to walk back to the top. We would take one exhausting step at a time through the heavy snow, being careful not to step in the track of our ski path.

Needless to say, there was never a fuss from any of us about going to sleep on those nights.

CHAPTER THREE

My First Real Home

My first real home was one of twenty company mill houses. It was my home for twenty-four years, and remained my parents' home until my father retired after forty-two years with Fraser.

Most of the mill houses were built alike and sixty feet apart. Ours had three bedrooms and was heated by a wood-burning (or coal) furnace in the cement-floored basement. The first floor was laid out with a kitchen, dining room and living room. There was also a shed room off the kitchen that opened to a back porch. The front porch was enclosed, but had windows that could be removed. Next to the house was a single, detached garage. The house and garage were repainted by the Fraser Company every five years.

Later, a second group of company houses was built on the southern side of Main Street, similar in size and design to ours. Their land area was more elevated than where we lived and adjacent to Picard's Field. My family's "neighborhood" included both these groups of company homes.

Our neighbors included the Drevers, the Camerons, the Roys, the Loves, the Johnsons, the Beaulieus, the Messecars, the Wylies, the Moores, the Heberts, the Cayers, the Kings, the

The Stewart home in Madawaska. I lived in this house from 1926 until 1950.

Kellys, the Watters, and the Seeleys. The small majority of English-speaking families in Madawaska occupied the Fraser company homes. Most of these families were unable to speak French, even those with French-sounding names.

The Beaulieus, for example, came from Wisconsin and did not speak French. The children of the neighborhood in time became bilingual. Many, like myself, were able to understand what was being said in French, but unfortunately, we were not able to speak it fluently. However, we learned enough to make ourselves understood, and as we grew older, speaking French became more manageable—even though there were many who never captured the beautiful-sounding accents, or expressions that sounded so much more romantic in French than they did in English.

Other than French, English, Scotch and Irish, there were no other ethnic groups in the area during the 1930s. There was only one Native American family that I knew, and later in high school, I befriended their son, Harold Bernard. He was the oldest boy in the Bernard family, and he often visited my home.

As children, all of us in the neighborhood enjoyed activities in Picard's Field. When I was a boy, Abel Picard was a bachelor farmer. He was short and wiry with a small peaked nose that he rubbed constantly during the winter months with his darkened leathered gloves, discolored by the reins that he held tightly as he guided his team of horses over the streets of Madawaska and Edmundston. In addition to farming, Mr. Picard was our iceman. During the winter, he cut blocks of ice from the frozen St. John River and made deliveries to our homes and many other neighborhoods in the town. The ice was placed in our icebox, which had chrome latched doors and an opening at the top. Mr. Picard would carry a block of ice into our kitchen using a large set of tongs. He was very accommodating: before placing the ice, he would run the block under the sink's water faucet to remove the sawdust.

He was even more accommodating to the children of our neighborhood. He would allow us to jump onto the back of his horse-drawn sled and ride with him on his delivery route. The bells attached to the horses' bridles would jingle and the sled runners would squeak over the hardened snow in the streets, flattening the droppings that the horses would leave along the way. With the back-and-forth motion of the sled, the blocks of ice would bump against each other causing small pieces to chip off. We would take the fallen chips, rub the sawdust off on our jackets, and quickly pop them into our mouths, cooling our tongues to match the temperature of the day.

Mr. Picard, who spoke very little English, would command the horses with guttural sounds in French, mixed with his limited vocabulary in English: "gee," "haw," "giddy-yap" and "whoa." At times, he would speak loudly, and at other times his voice was just above a whisper. The horses would respond accordingly, turning one way or the other, quickly or gently.

As young children, we giggled a lot as we rode with him, especially when the horses relieved themselves, causing us to pinch our noses as the odor wafted to the back of the sled. Mr. Picard had the same aroma about his clothing, but we didn't mind, or pinch our noses. Mr. Picard was our friend.

Chapter Four

Skating, Skiing, Sliding

As a young boy, the winters provided me with many more memorable times than other seasons did. Ice skating was the community's most popular pastime for both young and old. The Fraser Company had constructed outdoor rinks at various locations in Edmundston and Madawaska. Each rink was provided with a warming hut to spell the numbness of toes, fingers and faces of skaters affected by the frigid air.

I learned to skate on one such rink that was within a half-mile of my new home. Both my mother and father skated with me. They would hold me in balance night after night until I was able to stand alone without falling. In time, after many falls, bumps and bruises, I was able to skate around the rink on my own without holding onto the sideboards. Once I learned to do this, and how to change directions, I literally spent every evening, often without my parents, skating with my friends at the rink.

When the temperatures dropped to 10 and 20 degrees below zero Fahrenheit, as they did on many evenings, I still skated. As soon as I could feel the chill, I would enter the warming hut and sit as close as possible to the potbelly stove, which an attendant kept banked with coal. Soon, I'd be warm enough to get outside and skate again, until the cold sent me back into the hut to be warmed once more.

The Fraser rinks were open only in the evenings, but there were many patches of ice in town that allowed us to skate during the day as well, and we did. Snowstorms often covered our rinks, but they never stopped us from getting together after school with shovels to clear the areas and resume our skating activities.

It wasn't long after learning to skate that the boys acquired hockey sticks. We began playing "shinny" hockey as soon as we got out of school in the afternoon until it was time to go home for supper. A new fantasy took shape in our lives: We would play in the National Hockey League as soon as we were old enough. Many of us would emulate someone in the hockey world and whiz around the ice, dreaming we were that hockey hero.

I dreamed that I was Gordie Drillon, and I think others did as well. He was well known in the Maritime Provinces of Canada, having played for the Moncton (New Brunswick) Hawks, and later reaching stardom with the Toronto (Ontario) Maple Leafs. Hockey was the sport for boys. Baseball was the favorite national sport and pastime of the United States, but it never attracted the interest that hockey did in the Land of the Porcupine.

After a heavy downfall of snow, it could take days to clear the ice rinks. Our attention would then be diverted to sliding. Most every child in the area who was old enough to slide owned a Speed-a-way sled, made by the Paris Manufacturing Company in Norway, Maine (although that wasn't all important, nor did we care, at the time). We just knew that a Speed-a-way could out-slide any other make, and it would fly down the hills of Madawaska. When the flat runners on the standard Speed-a-way were replaced with round runners, the sled was even faster!

Sledding on the streets of Madawaska was forbidden—and for good reason—but we did it anyway. The town is built on a sloping hill, with the majority of the streets running from the height of the land on the south side of the town to the St. John River, on the north side. Main Street runs parallel with the river, and the sliding hills that we elected to use crossed Main Street or terminated at Main Street. Automobiles were not plentiful in the '30s, but Main Street nevertheless was the main route through town, and to cross Main Street from the south side to the north side on a sled was hazardous. Very few of us paid heed to this risk as we zoomed down the snow-packed streets, racing each other to the bottom.

We learned that the more weight the sled carried, the faster it would travel. Often we would double up, with the driver lying flat on his stomach and a friend kneeling on the back of the sled with head tucked forward and into the back of the driver to minimize any wind friction. Winning those downhill races was very important to us, so we would devise any means possible to increase our speed. We were ecstatic when one of the older boys in the neighborhood would agree to ride with us, knowing that the extra weight he carried assured us of being the first to reach the bottom of the hill. A competitive spirit was developing at a very young age.

As I reflect on those times, I find it surprising that our parents never lectured us about the danger of crossing Main Street in the darkness of early evening. I suspect that they never gave much thought to it, believing that we knew better, or that we were sliding in the fields and off the streets. As children, we never considered that we were in danger or thought that we were doing anything illegal. Our one-man police force knew, however. He constantly warned us and sent us home on many evenings with a threat that we would be arrested if we didn't cease and desist.

Apparently, our parents were never notified that we were violating the "no sledding on town streets" regulation, which, as I realized later, was probably only an unofficial policy. The threats of arrest had little effect on us for some reason, and we continued to violate the rule, which had never been enacted by a town ordinance, returning to the same sliding hills again and again, compelled by the thrill of a speeding sled and the thrill of winning.

Chapter Five

Radio Entertainment

There were many nights in northern Maine during the winter months when the temperature dropped well below zero degrees Fahrenheit, and with a chilling wind factor, it became unbearable to be outside for sledding, skating or for carving out snow caves. On such nights, it was prudent to stay indoors and enjoy the comfort of a hot-air furnace that brought warmth through black square registers in the floors of every room in the house. On evenings when the wind blew heavily and drafts were felt throughout the house no matter how much the furnace had been stoked, we often stood directly over the registers and enjoyed the heat as it wafted over our bodies toward the ceiling.

Television had not yet been invented, so radio was our entertainment when we were confined indoors. Those nights were memorable as we strained to hear our favorite programs through the static created by the aurora borealis or northern lights. My father would have his listening time interrupted as he continuously checked the furnace in the cellar, adding wood or coal, to be sure that the house temperature remained comfortable, while my mother would check the tea kettle in the kitchen to be sure it didn't boil dry, and to refill her cup with fresh-brewed Red Rose tea.

The northern lights phenomena appeared regularly during the winter months, and became truly bothersome to our radio reception. As the sound "cracked," and then faded out, I would press closer to our Atwater Kent radio to hear the latest episodes of *Little Orphan Annie*, *Jack Armstrong, the All-American Boy*, or *Bobby Benson on the H-Bar-O Ranch*, sponsored by the Hecker H-O Company. Many of these programs that caught the fancy of the young listener were sponsored by breakfast food companies.

These companies offered giveaways that kept me glued to the radio from one episode to the next. *Little Orphan Annie* was sponsored by Ovaltine, which offered a variety of Orphan Annie milk shakers and a metal disc that I recall could be used to decipher secret code messages that were transmitted through the radio program. There were many more items that I was able to obtain by forwarding the silver seal removed from the top of an Ovaltine container. Photographs of Bobby Benson and other cowboys of the H-Bar-O Ranch could be obtained by sending box tops from Hecker H-O Company. The Ralston Cereal Company sponsored the *Tom Mix* show, and as if it were yesterday, I can recall the wonderful gifts that were supplied through their program in return for box tops. I especially remember the full-size wooden replica of Tom Mix's pistol. It was simply beautiful and one of my most prized possessions for years.

Radio not only provided us with entertainment, it sharpened the imagination of the young listener. We visualized the creaking door as the Shadow spoke. We could see the rain and the streaks of lightning as we heard the claps of thunder. We could imagine the Lone Ranger and Tonto riding off into the horizon simply by listening to the sound of hoofbeats ebbing to an inaudible level, and the distant cry of "Hi Ho, Silver." And, when Fibber McGee opened his closet door, we could immediately see the pots, pans, dishes, and other items that we knew were stuffed in our own closets, tumbling outward. Henceforth, people generally referred to their own messy closets as Fibber McGee's closet.

Radio also brought us our sports. My father was an avid sports fan, so I was allowed to stay up much later than usual when a major sports event was being broadcast, and I was always allowed to listen when Joe Louis was defending his world championship boxing title. I stayed up when Hockey Night in Canada was on, and Foster Hewitt brought us the play-by-play of the games played in Maple Leaf Garden in Toronto. The show was sponsored by Imperial Oil Company of Canada. We listened intently, hoping that Syl Apps or Gordie Drillon would score.

We were greatly disappointed whenever the signal from Toronto was too weak for us to hear the game well. On one occasion when this happened during the Stanley Cup play-offs, my father immediately told me to get dressed for outdoors, which I did (but wondered why). We walked across the bridge to Edmundston, to the Canadian Telegraph Office, where others had already gathered, apparently having the same reception problems that we had experienced. The progress of the game was being received by teletype. It was just like being there, as the telegrapher read the tape and announced who had scored to the assembled hockey fans. If the favored team had scored, a loud cheer went up, and very soon afterwards we would learn who had assisted. An odd way to listen to a hockey game, to be sure; but the memories of such enjoyable nights are precious, as they will never be realized again.

By including me in his passionate love of these games, my father instilled in me a great love of hockey and other sports. Seventy years later, I still have those same emotions and get as excited as ever when I sit in the stands of an arena and watch, or view on television, a good hockey game.

Chapter Six

First Year of School, Mud Season

When I turned six, I began school—but the school was in Canada, not the United States. I started school in Edmundston and graduated from Edmundston High School in 1942.

There were good reasons why I was educated in Canada instead of the United States. First, because my parents and I were all born in Canada, they wanted me to be schooled there. The most important reason, however, may have been the lack of an established school system in Madawaska when I was ready to enter school. I was told that, at the time, the first-grade class (which I would have attended that first year) was held in the local barbershop in Madawaska. I have never been able to confirm whether or not this was true.

I have tried to recall memories of my very first day in school in 1931, but I cannot. The distance between my home and the Academy, as the school was known, was approximately one mile. Every day I had to walk across the long International Bridge to school. I can't believe that on that first day I walked the mile to school by myself. My mother must have taken me, but I have no recollection of this being the case. I'm certain that she comforted me and tried to alleviate my concerns by talking to me about how much fun school would be, how I would learn to read, write, and add numbers, and how I would meet many new friends. I was a very shy boy at age six, and her words must have removed the many anxieties I had of attending school for the first time. I have to believe that she came back to the school and walked me home on that first day. I walked alone on many other days, but sometimes walked with an older girl from my neighborhood.

My new school was a two-story brick building with a sidewalk in front. A large play area to one side of the building was completely enclosed by a gray wooden fence. On the opposite side of the play area was the local post office, a large brick building with a bell tower over the main entrance. Across the street from the school was a small diner that had a bright figure of "Wimpy" painted on the outside of its front door. Wimpy, a character from the *Popeye* comic strip, was shown munching on a hamburger, his favorite food.

The school was public but administered by an order of Catholic nuns, and while it was non-parochial, prayers were said daily before class. My first-grade teacher was the young Miss Miller. I remember her especially well from the embarrassment she caused me when I became attracted to a tiny blonde girl named Lois Hutchison. I had selected her as my first girlfriend, although I doubt if Lois ever suspected my feelings for her. Whatever possessed me is beyond explanation, but during recess one morning I decided to kiss Lois—and the first kiss that I had ever given to anyone, other than to my parents, was witnessed by Miss Miller.

When we returned to our classroom seats, Miss Miller went to the front of the room, looked straight at me, and said, "Ronald, did I see you kiss Lois in the schoolyard a few minutes ago?" My face turned red, and as I stared at the floor, I said nothing in reply.

At age eight, I'm about to cross the International Bridge between Madawaska and Edmundston, New Brunswick. I crossed the bridge four times daily while attending school in Canada for eleven years.

She continued with, "I believe that you should apologize to Lois for your boldness, don't you agree?"

I kept staring at the floor and my face reddened even more, but I didn't apologize because I didn't know what to say. My face remained a bright rose color for the rest of the week. That first kiss of mine has been remembered by me as one of the most embarrassing moments in my life, although I have had other awkward times since first grade.

Discipline was very strict at the Academy School. The principal was the Sister Superior, a frail, graying nun who wore silver-rimmed glasses that rested on the tip of her narrow, peaked nose. A three-inch cross hung down the front of her gray habit. She was short, small, and a mousy type of woman, with eyes that showed little emotion or compassion. Misbehaving students were sent to her office, and Sister Superior decided on the punishment. Very quickly and with few words, she would open the top drawer of her desk, remove a fifteen-inch leather strap, and coldly say to the offending student, "Put out your hand, palm upward."

I misbehaved one day and was sent to Sister Superior's office. I entered and stood petrified before her desk. She said what I expected her to say, as other students had told me how their punishments went. "Put out your hand, palm upward," she said. With hand extended, the strap came down across my palm with a loud *whack!* I can still recall the pain as she repeatedly hit my palm, as many times as she thought the severity of my classroom behavior required. For some reason, I didn't cry. The punishment could be considered cruel, but it was effective. I never wanted to return to her office for a second time, and I never did.

My first year of school went by quickly as I made new friends in my first grade class. The walk back and forth to school on many January and February mornings was no easy chore, especially when crossing the bridge. Because of the bridge's openness to the St. John River and the prevailing winds that followed the river downwind, the temperature on the bridge often dropped to a low of 40 degrees below zero. My mother protected me from these freezing temperatures by pulling the tabs of my hat down over my ears, buttoning my coat to the very top and wrapping a wool scarf around my neck and over the lower part of my face, leaving only my eyes exposed. My breath through the scarf would build up moisture on the outside of the woolen material and freeze, causing my eyebrows to be covered with ice. On many mornings I had to walk backwards across the bridge so that the brunt of the cold wind wouldn't hit me head-on. When the weather was real severe, my mother would arrange for me to eat at a lunch counter in Edmundston rather than come home at noon.

As March wound down, the sun got higher in the sky and the air warmed. The snowbanks began to crystallize and crumble. In April, the first signs of thawing snow began to flow in the streets, and frost came out of the frozen soil, making the roads throughout the St. John Valley impassable. Spring was known as the mud season.

It was also the season when our young bodies wanted to run through puddles and float sticks and other boat-like objects in roadside ditches filled with water from the melting snow. It was a time of year for muddy shoes and boots and wet socks. It was also the time of year when we caught colds and our parents would rub camphor on our chests underneath our undershirts. In our classrooms, the air was permeated with the smells of camphor and the odors of wet woolen coats, scarves and mittens set to dry on heat registers.

Spring was the season for marbles, and schoolyards became high activity areas for marble playing. We would arrive early and play before classes started and continue our games through recess. Often we would meet after school and play before we headed for home. By spring, I had made friends with three boys my age—Gerald Leaman, Vance Toner and Bobby Murchie. These friends were all English-speaking, and for that reason we separated ourselves from those of French descent, although all of us got along well in school. It was just easier to communicate when we all spoke the same language.

We four had a good supply of marbles, and the competition to win as many as we could from those we competed against was always very keen. There were clay marbles and "glassies." The clay marbles were messy because the dye would run and stain our hands and clothing whenever they got wet. It was impossible to keep them dry, so daily I had blue, yellow and green stains on my hands, on the inside of my pockets, on my coat, pants, and mittens. My mother would scold me, but it did little good as we continued to play marbles throughout most of the spring—with clay marble stains prevailing on my clothes.

To win clay marbles was no great prize as they were less expensive to buy, so more of them were used. The real prize was the glassie, as they were made of clear glass with swirling clouds of various colors on the inside. They varied in size, and the larger "shooter glassie" was the sought-after treasure. They differed in design and were absolutely beautiful with their varied color combinations. To win a glassie from an opponent brought an immediate high and sense of exhilaration to the young player, but to lose brought an equally intense sadness and disappointment.

As we chose up sides to play marbles, we had to decide who would play first. We had ways of doing this other than tossing a coin, because few of us had coins to toss. We drew a circle in the mud and each tossed a marble in the direction of the circle. Whoever landed closest to the circle (or inside of the circle) got to play last. There was an advantage to playing last because you could "sight in" on your opponent's already tossed marble. I would hold the marble between my thumb and forefinger, close one eye, and sight in with the other eye, lining up the direction of flight that I wished the marble to take. As soon as the sighting operation was completed, I would extend my hand forward in the direction of the marble on the ground. It was an unwritten rule that one had to stand upright and not scoot down, or lean forward, which would reduce the distance that the marble had to travel before it was released.

If a shooter was successful enough to hit or tick the marble on the ground with his marble, the ticked marble became the possession of the shooter. If one missed, however, the roles of the two teams were reversed, and the contest continued.

Whoever had the good fortune of a keen eye—or some luck—on any given day would go home with a bagful of new marbles and a feeling of happiness. If, on the other hand, one experienced poor luck or a dull eye, that person would head for home from the schoolyard feeling much differently—especially if a favorite glassie had been lost.

My first year of school was more than learning to read, write, and do arithmetic. I learned to overcome shyness and to make new friends. School was interesting to me. I was curious about the large world that was located beyond my home. Being away from home all day during the week made me less dependent upon my parents, although I always enjoyed getting home in the afternoons and seeing my dog, Tony, a black-and-white bulldog, and joining my mother and father for our nightly conversations around the dinner table.

Chapter Seven

Summer Activities

Quite often the cold of winter would linger through the months of March, April, and May, and then suddenly warmer weather would arrive. With that signal, we children knew that shortly thereafter, school would be over for the year.

Summer was usually late in arriving. Nothing much grew in the St. John Valley until the middle of May. The valley seemed to lag a full month behind the growing season of southern Maine, but once the ground warmed, the trees, flowers and gardens all caught up to the rest of the state very quickly, and suddenly the open fields and wooded hillsides were lush, green, and as colorful as they were elsewhere.

The season offered me a new set of outdoor activities. It was a time to romp through the wooded areas at the edge of town to play cowboys and Indians. It was a time to play softball and baseball. It was a time to sell lemonade and hot dogs, to go bicycling, and to play a variety of backyard games like kick the can or Simon says. It was also a time to visit grandparents, cousins, aunts, and uncles.

Baseball was not as popular as hockey, but we played "sandlot" ball whenever we could assemble enough players to choose up teams. There was no Little League or other organized, adult-controlled sports. We simply gathered on some vacant lot and placed rocks on the four corners of the infield to mark the bases. Usually, the older boys acted as captains. They would first decide who would have the first pick of players by tossing a bat and overlapping one hand over the other up the bat until there was no space left at the top for another hand. The captain who won the last grip on the bat was then allowed to choose the first member of his team.

Some boys always played a little better than others, and they always got picked first. Others who didn't play well naturally got picked last. But, no matter how poorly some boys played, each one got picked and anyone who wanted to could play. I always got picked somewhere in the middle, and I don't recall ever having been picked last—but maybe that was because I owned the bat and the ball! At any rate, and for whatever reason, I played often and enjoyed the fun of those games that went on and on without any set number of innings, ending whenever we decided we had had enough or it was time to head home for a meal. As to who was the winner of the game, none of us really cared—we had fun and that was the main thing to us!

The upper heights south of Madawaska were heavily wooded. None of the residents within the town proper lived very far from a heavy growth of trees. Residential properties, as well as commercial properties and the Fraser Paper mill, had been constructed within a strip of land that ran east to west, parallel to the St. John River and the heightened land south of town.

The woods became our western frontier as we acted out the heroic antics of the favorite Western actors we had come to know and idolize at the movie house week after week. We might imagine ourselves to be Roy Rogers, Buck Jones or Tom Mix. I always favored Hop-a-long Cassidy, who was played by William Boyd in the movies. Whoever I pretended to be on any given day, I would race through the woods and stop to hide behind a stump or a large boulder and wait in ambush for a friend who had decided to play the part of an Indian. The Indian was the enemy, as they were continuously portrayed in the movies as savages and bad guys. Little did I know at the time, because no one ever told me, that many Native Americans were driven to savagery by broken treaties.

Being a cowboy was a young boy's dream, and I loved to gallop through the woods. I would clap my hand on the side of my hip and talk to my "horse" as he carried me down a wooded path in hot pursuit of an Indian, who I knew was only a short distance ahead. I would slow my horse down as I approached my object of pursuit and ready my cap pistol to fire upon sight. What imaginations we had, and what pleasure we received as we daily ignited those limitless imaginations.

Our developing minds were not always inclined to the world of fantasy. On extremely warm days, our thoughts were directed toward money. So we became entrepreneurs and usually sold lemonade, Kool-Aid or other cold drinks, and sometimes even hot dogs, to the mill workers who came off the day shift at four p.m.

Cold drinks were always an immediate sellout, as the papermakers had been sweltering under the heat of the paper machines for eight hours.

The capital investment for our start-up expenses came from our parents. One of us would borrow a dollar, which we immediately spent at Gardner's store on Main Street on a couple packs of Kool-Aid, a pound or two of hot dogs, and some buns. We would then go home to get ice and cook the hot dogs. Just before four o'clock, we would borrow a card table, place our wares on it, and put up a "lemonade and hot dogs for sale" sign. Then we'd wait for the mill traffic to walk along Mill Street.

How we figured the mark-up on our sale items, I can't recall, but we always profited sufficiently to provide us with enough money for the weekend movie and a bag of popcorn. Since the price of the Saturday afternoon movie was a nickel, our business profits must have been marginal.

We never missed the Saturday matinees at the Star Theatre in Edmundston. Movies had a special attraction for all of us, not so much because of the excitement created by Roy Rogers, Gene Autry, or other well-known cowboy actors at that time, but more for the serials that were part of the afternoon entertainment. These adventurous episodes with their futuristic visions ran for about fifteen minutes following the main feature. The heroes were explorers of space, such as Buck Rogers or Flash Gordon. Each serial, being advanced science fiction stories, featured rocket ships, laser beams, and visual talking machines (which looked very much like the public pay phones of today, but with a screen built into the face of the box allowing the person making the call to see the person receiving the call). The serials also allowed us to visit persons living in the cities of outer space, dressed in clothing much different than ours of today, and living with amenities uncommon to our living standards at this time. Many of the visionary objects that stretched our imaginations beyond belief when we saw them on the screen in the mid-1930s have become realities in today's world. And how those serials kept us in suspense! Each story covered fifteen weeks, with each episode finding our hero in some inescapable situation at the end, from which there was seemingly no visible escape. Each segment left us anxious about what next week's episode would bring. By some miracle, however, during the next episode, a solution to our hero's dilemma was found, and he escaped unharmed.

Chapter Eight

Family Reunions

Summer meant visiting grandparents in New Brunswick. It also brought me together with my urban cousins in Saint John and my country cousins in St. George. I enjoyed being with both groups, but they were quite different in their interests.

As for grandparents, I liked my grandfather Stewart and grandmother Conway the best. My father's father, whom we called "Pa," was a perky and wiry little fellow, whose back was bent over considerably from working in the fields. He lived and farmed in St. George for the greater part of his life. As a young man, he served for a short time as a crew member on a sailing vessel that fished for cod off the coast of Newfoundland.

Pa had a deep voice for a small man, and used to roar at my cousin Lawrence and me when he caught us in his garden pulling up carrots or stuffing our faces with new peas. He wasn't as gruff as he seemed, but was in fact a very compassionate person. He was bald when we knew him, except for heavy sideburns of silver, but it was his eyes that captured attention. They glimmered with an expectancy of tomfoolery, and I suspect that at one time in his life he was a hellion—although according to my father, Pa had never taken a drink of alcohol or smoked in his life. My father also claimed that never once had he ever heard Pa utter a swear word,

My grandfather, William Wallace Stewart, and my grandmother, Ada (McCready) Stewart, at their home in St. George, New Brunswick.

although I did once hear him call his horse a "bitch" on an afternoon that I rode into town with him, and it surprised me greatly.

Pa loved to have company. On Sunday afternoons he would often invite members from the congregation of the Baptist church to join him in his parlor where his granddaughter Ruth would play the piano, and everyone would join in the singing of hymns. He would loudly sing, "Are your garments white; are they white as snow; are you blessed in the blood of the lamb?" His eyes would glitter with joy and contentment, and he would end by laughing out loud to show his happiness.

Throughout his life, Pa never owned an automobile. He had a team of horses that he would drive into town every Saturday evening, a distance of about three miles from his home. In later years, when he no longer owned horses, he continued his visits to town on Saturday evenings, walking both ways. In town, he would stand on a corner of Main Street, near Dewar's store, chat with friends or strangers for two or three hours, and then return home.

He was an active man throughout his farming days, maintaining a large garden that extended the full length of a half-mile lane that led to his farm off the Manor Road in St. George. In the evenings, when the work was done, and as tired as he may have been, he would sit and enjoy a large plate of homemade baked beans, a cup of tea, and three or four of my grandmother's molasses or oatmeal cookies before he went to bed. He was well past eighty at the time, but apparently eating before going to bed never bothered him, and he lived to the ripe old age of ninety-two.

I always loved going to Pa's farm when I was a young boy. We usually went over the Fourth of July holiday. I couldn't wait to arrive at the head of his lane and see the white farmhouse on the right and the large red barn on the left. Often I would catch sight of my grandfather working on the roof of the barn or scooting around the yard doing chores. My father would blow the car horn and Pa would look back up the lane to see who was coming.

Although we couldn't hear him, he must have let out a holler, because before we reached the farmhouse, he and my grandmother, "Ma," and my cousin, Ruth, who lived with them, were out on the porch to greet us.

If we arrived for a visit after Pa had left for his Saturday night visit to town, my father and I would drive into the village, park the car, and walk down Main Street toward where we knew we would find him, chatting with friends. As we approached him, we would slow our pace. Then, ambling in front of him, my father would say, "Good evening, Mr. Stewart." His father, not immediately recognizing us, would reply with a quick "Good evening," but then as he saw us his face would light up with a wide smile, spreading his handlebar moustache across his face, his arms wide apart to embrace each of us.

My grandmother Stewart never warmed up to me and I never felt as close to her as I did to Pa. She never showed compassion to my cousins who lived nearby, either, so apparently it was just her nature. But she was always hospitable and always seemed happy to see my parents and me during our summer visits.

Ma was a wonderful cook, and it only seemed like minutes after we arrived that her dining room table was set for some of the most memorable meals I can recall in my lifetime. She would have new potatoes fresh from my grandfather's garden and sweet peas served with Saint John Harbor salmon as our meal for each Fourth of July visit. The meal was a tradition to celebrate Canada's Dominion Day, which falls on July 1, but our Canadian Stewart relatives always combined the two holidays for our family reunions. Fresh buttermilk was served, and the meal was topped off with molasses and oatmeal cookies, all homemade by Ma. They were my favorites then and remain so to this day.

All of the vegetables served on those summer visits were seasoned with butter that Ma had churned and salted, resulting in flavored vegetables that were unsurpassed. I would eat and eat, until my then-skinny little body was stretched to a point of discomfort. I'm sure that if I had visited the entire summer with my grandparents, I would have developed into a butterball. My frailty was certainly no fault of Grandmother Stewart's.

My father's only brother, Wilfred—who everyone called "Buck"—lived on the farm next to my grandparents. Shortly after we settled in for our visit, Buck and his family would join us. He and his wife, Ethel, had six girls and one boy. After salutations were completed, all of us would gather in the dining room and the stories would begin. My father and his brother would try to outdo the other with the biggest lies they could imagine. Most of their exaggerated stories were about hunting or fishing, or other events that they recalled from their earlier years. The same stories would be repeated year after year, and my cousins and I would sit listening, giggling, and wondering if we should believe what we were hearing.

Buck's favorite stories were about when he had pitched for the local town baseball team. And, according to my father, some of the stories about a string of strikeouts were not all that exaggerated. Buck still loved to pitch, and it wouldn't be too long on the second day of our visit before both children and adults were playing ball in the field next to Pa's barn. Even my mother joined in on the fun. Only my grandmother and grandfather sat out the game, but occasionally my grandfather came off the front porch and attempted to hit one of Buck's mighty pitches.

Buck was always the pitcher in these games, and constantly heckled us as he went into a long, drawn-out windup. None of us ever expected to hit his fastball and stood at the plate in semi-fear. But it was all for show, and when Buck would come out of his overemphasized windup, the ball came at us slowly, and in most instances we were able to hit it. When we did hit the ball, there were loud screams and yells as we raced around the bases knowing that we had outsmarted one of St. George's greatest pitchers.

Buck's son, Lawrence, was the only boy cousin on my father's side of the family, and we have remained close over the years. He has been a surrogate brother to me, since I had none. We often reflect on those wonderful days when parents and children played together and learned to love one another as a family.

After our visit during the Fourth of July was over, we would return to Madawaska. Shortly thereafter, my mother and I would visit her parents, brothers, and sisters in Saint John, N.B. We would usually spend two or three weeks with them at a rented cottage, and my father would join us later for a week of his vacation time. We would leave from Edmundston by train and travel through Grand Falls, Woodstock and Fredericton, arriving at the Fairville Station several hours later. We were always met by my grandfather Conway, who had a love for trains, even though earlier in his life he had become severely handicapped as a result of a train accident.

My grandmother, Clara (Shaw) Conway of Fairville, New Brunswick.

My mother's family lived only a short distance from the station, so we walked to their house. I would run ahead of my mother and grandfather, as grandmother Conway was one of my favorite people and I was always excited to see her. "Nannie" was quite different from my grandmother Stewart. She was very attentive, and upon seeing me would hold me in her arms, hugging me firmly and whispering how she had missed me and loved me. She was a large woman, and as far back as I can remember, she would complain about lameness in her knees. Her knees were large and swollen, requiring her to walk with a cane. She wore small, gold-rimmed glasses at the end of a very small pug nose, always reminding me of Mrs. Santa Claus. She had deviltry in her eyes, though, and sometimes I wondered how lame she really was. When my father visited later in the summer, he and my Uncle Freeman would occasionally have an alcoholic drink, and when they did, they always offered Nannie one. She would always accept and shortly thereafter would forget her lameness. She'd lift up from the rocking chair, which she occupied a good part of the day, or if standing, throw her cane down and do an Irish jig. She was something else!

My grandfather Conway was Irish through and through, always referring to "me hat," or "me coat," and was full of the blarney as anyone could be. He was a short, roly-poly type, with a huge stomach and a walrus-type mustache. He would talk for hours with anyone who would listen, and seemed to know everyone that ever lived around Fairville. Everyone knew him, too. He was easily recognizable because he always wore a three-piece dress suit with one sleeve tucked into a pocket of the coat. He lost his right arm when he worked as a trainman for the Canadian National Railway. After the accident, the railroad employed him as gate attendant at the Fairville Crossing, and he held that position for years. He became a familiar sight in the area, always welcoming the opportunity to provide strangers with directions or local gossip, or to converse on whatever subject matter others would share with him.

My visits to Saint John offered me the companionship of many cousins. It wasn't long after I visited with Nannie that I would head out across the field to see my Aunt Jo and her three children. Jo would know when we were coming and have fresh-baked banana bread ready to be sliced. She would butter it for me and, with pleasure on her face, watch me devour this special treat in a matter of seconds. To this day, my Aunt Jo's banana bread is the best that I've ever tasted. I've never been sure whether my eagerness to visit my aunt's house related to her banana bread or to her three children, who became my summer companions when my mother and I were in the city of Saint John.

During the summer month away from my father, my mother rented a small cottage next to the golf course in Bayside, a short distance from Saint John. We visited the city often, and I'd play with my cousins. Aunt Jo had two girls and a boy, the oldest girl being my age, so she and I spent considerable time together. My mother had another sister, Aunt Dube, who had two boys and a girl at the time (she had a fourth child much later in life). Although her oldest child was a boy, I spent most of my playtime with her only daughter, and this friendship has continued into our adult lives.

As much as I enjoyed my cousins' companionship when my mother visited with her sisters, I was more content to stay at the cottage, spending my daylight hours walking the edge of the fairways picking up golf balls. It was like looking for treasure, and I would get excited every time that I found one, eagerly awaiting the arrival of my father, so I could present him with my "booty" of golf balls, which would exceed a hundred count by the time he arrived. He would express surprise on my good fortune, and his thankful acceptance of my "gift" always left me feeling proud with the sense that my days of diligent search through tall grass, rocks, crevices, trees, and alder bushes were not wasted, although I thought the time spent was play and not work.

My father, of course, shared the golf balls with me, and we played golf every day of his vacation. As a result, the total find was greatly reduced by the end of the second week of play. I lost nearly as many as I found, and my father wasn't always in the fairway, either. He was a pretty average golfer, not being exceptionally long off the tee but most of the time down the center of the fairway and very accurate within 100 yards of the pin. What he lacked in distance, he made up on the greens, and always putted extremely well. He was a "bogey" golfer, although occasionally he scored better. My father always showed uncharacteristic patience while playing golf, and I have often wondered about that. My father taught me the game of golf, and I have enjoyed it throughout my life.

My mother was a compulsive shopper. Before my father would arrive for his vacation time, my mother would spend many of our summer afternoons in the city, insisting that I tag along, not wanting to leave me at the cottage alone. We would board the electric trolley in Fairville and ride to the square at the head of King Street in Saint John. We would walk the entire length of King Street to Dock Street, an historical site where the Loyalists landed long ago.

We entered every store and "mooched," as my mother called it, over the merchandise. I promised not to be fussy if my mother agreed that we would visit the City Market before the day was ended. The City Market was then—and is still—my favorite place in Saint John. It was a large, airy structure that sloped at about a five-degree angle from one end to the other, taking in the length of a city block. It bustled with activity, being visited daily by farmers with newly picked vegetables from their fertile farmlands bordering the Kennebecasis River. Dairymen brought fresh butter and cheeses from the Sussex area. Fishermen arrived daily with fresh catches from the Bay of Fundy or silver salmon caught in Saint John Harbor. The freshly picked vegetables, cut flowers, and salty fish mixed with the pungent smell of freshly cut dulse, a form of dried seaweed for those with an acquired taste, and filled the air with aromatic ambrosia.

Except for a few structural improvements, the market hasn't changed significantly in the past seventy years that I have been visiting it. Bins line the outer edges and the center lane of the market and are filled daily with dulse, vegetables, freshly cut meats, fish, dried flowers, hand-carved wooden figures, and a variety of local crafts. Freshly killed chickens still hang from hooks, and occasionally, rabbits are sold. Bright red cuts of newly slaughtered beef and pork line the refrigerated showcases. Canadian cheeses, from mild to extra strong, are cut from large rounds and sold by hardy-looking vendors with grimy fingernails wearing stained aprons. I have never visited the market without making a purchase, nor did my mother when I shopped with her in those early days of my youth.

I could hardly wait to get back to our cottage in Bayside to enjoy a large hunk of very old and very strong cheese on a saltine cracker, washed down with a steaming cup of Red Rose tea, which I was allowed to have at an early age. I also enjoyed placing strips of freshly picked dulse on top of a warm woodstove until it became green, crispy, and crunchy. When cooked on the stove, dulse loses its strong medicinal taste and becomes more palatable. I still like the taste of it, cooked or uncooked—two distinctly different tastes. When eaten uncooked, dulse, a leafy sea vegetable with red, wedge-shaped fronds, has a salty, medicinal taste. When cooked, however, the leaves turn green and the dulse is crispy—much more tasty.

My mother loved to shop, and although I preferred to stay at the cottage and search the course for golf balls, I have to admit that I enjoyed her shopping sprees. The days in the city passed too quickly as we wandered from jewelry shops to five-and-ten-cent stores to a park bench in King Square at the top of King Street to sit and feed the pigeons. I was fascinated by the fog that blew in from the harbor, silhouetting the sailors dressed in their dark blue bell-bottoms and pure white-rimmed hats against the skyline of Saint John. As I watched, I imagined the experiences and adventures that these uniformed men must have encountered while at sea. At a young age I became determined that one day I would be a sailor. When World War II broke out in 1939, it wasn't long before my childhood dreams became a reality.

When my mother and I finished our shopping lark, we would board the electric trolley and ride back to Fairville. I would run to the opposite end of the trolley and sit where the conductor sat when he brought the trolley to Saint John. I would imagine that I was the conductor, turning the shiny brass lever of the steering mechanism, which somehow activated the electrical wire over the trolley tracks. When the conductor changed positions from one end of the trolley to the other, he would immediately activate one end of the trolley and deactivate the other end. I never understood how this was done, but it did allow me to pretend from the deactivated end that I was the conductor, and that I was responsible for moving the trolley to its destination. I would turn the lever in a complete rotation and reverse directions very much like the conductor did when he wished to accelerate or slow the vehicle to a stop. I often wondered why the conductors allowed me to sit in their seat, but I expect they sensed my enjoyment, and my presence provided no hindrance to the trolley's operation. They would always pleasantly say good-bye as we disembarked, and I would sheepishly smile back, feeling somewhat embarrassed that I really hadn't helped the conductor at all in getting the trolley car safely to its destination.

Chapter Nine

Nighthawks, Bats and Death

Following our annual visits with my grandparents, I returned home on the train to Edmundston with my mother and looked forward to the remaining weeks of summer vacation. There was never a lack of ideas as to what I could do with my time away from school. I was an extremely active and curious child.

As a young boy, I especially enjoyed watching wildlife in the forested area south of town and the numerous species of birds that visited our neighborhood. I found great pleasure resting my back on the warm grass of the lawn, often for more than an hour at a time, looking skyward to watch nighthawks gather insects. I was awed by their swooping dives, their long pointed wings pulled back, exposing white patches on their outer wings as they fell straight down toward earth. As the distance to the ground lessened, they suddenly reversed direction, zooming upwards and emitting a loud buzzing, which sounded like *peent, peent*. They were particularly active just before nightfall, and the upward climbs and downward swoops would go on for hours.

Some evenings while watching the birds with friends in my neighborhood, we'd see large planes flying overhead, and we wondered where they were going. We were aware that events in

Europe were causing our parents concern, and the name Hitler was frequently mentioned in their conversations. We were also seeing pictures of military activities on the Pathe newsreels, which preceded our Saturday afternoon movies. The weekly newsreels were how we became familiar with German Stuka dive-bombers. We would talk about them as we watched the nighthawks, with our young imaginations changing the nighthawks into German bombers and yelling out very loudly, "bombs away," as the birds swooped down over the ground and continued upwards, not really knowing who or what our imaginary Stukas had targeted.

Bats, as we watched them flutter around the neighborhood streetlights, were also a curiosity to my young friends and me. We feared them. We believed the stories of Dracula and kept our distance from them. We feared that should they ever get caught in our hair, we were doomed.

One day, I was hiding behind my father's garage during a game of hide-and-seek. I realized I was standing on a flat board and, for whatever reason, lifted the board off the ground. As I did, a dark black wing spread its full width sideways, and at the same time a small fox-like face, baring small sharp teeth, stared upwards at me. It was a bat, and I was petrified! I dropped the board and ran into the house as quickly as I could get through the door. Trembling, I wrapped my arms around my mother. For several nights afterwards, I had trouble getting to sleep, and asked my mother to sit with me. I couldn't get the vision out of my mind—those bared teeth and that fox-like face with dark beady eyes staring at me. The image returned on several nights, as I thought how close I had come to being doomed.

The bat experience occurred during a period of time in my childhood when I was having frequent nightmares, brought on by experiences that left me with fearful impressions. I had a serious problem overcoming one nightmare that started after I had witnessed death for the first time. The Kelly family, who lived three houses away from me, had a two-month-old girl who suddenly died. The children in the neighborhood visited their home. It was the first time that I had ever seen a dead person. Her body was in a small white casket, seemingly no larger than a shoebox, resting on a table in their dining room. The image of that child remains with me until this day. She was so small and peaceful looking. Her soft white hands and arms were folded across her narrow chest, covered with a beautiful white-laced frock. I gazed at her intently and wondered what it was like to die. And why so young? It was hard for me to turn away from her closed eyes, which appeared to stare at me. Many strange thoughts bothered me as I dreamt about that angelic face for weeks, wondering if she was now in heaven, if there really was such a place.

Three years later, I experienced death for the second time when a fourth-grade classmate died of a ruptured intestine. I did not want to see another person my age in death, but the teacher insisted that the entire class attend the funeral as a group. I begged my mother to excuse me from school on the day of the funeral, but she thought it best that I attend with the others, and I did. As I passed the casket, again I was bothered and disturbed.

My deceased classmate was taller and larger than I was, although we were both the same age of nine years. I thought to myself, why did he die? To me, death seemed to be a terrible thing, and I dreamt of him often after the funeral. I would awake from fearful nightmares that he was in my bedroom. My mother would again have to sit with me as I struggled to go back to sleep with images of death filling my mind.

Chapter Ten

Potatoes, Hunting and Halloween

Summer always seemed to be so short. The days suddenly became cooler as Labor Day passed, and I had to ready myself to return to school. The Edmundston schools, which I attended, opened shortly after Labor Day, but Madawaska schools remained closed because it was potato-picking time in Aroostook County. Children of school age were hired to harvest the potato crop, which was important for the economy of the County. I seldom picked except for a few times on the weekends, and it was not my favorite entrepreneurial experience.

Picking started early in the morning. Pickers assembled at a convenient location and then were driven off in a farmer's truck to a field that might be several miles away. Once picked up, we were committed for the entire day with no means of returning. The time of pickup was usually before the sun had risen over the horizon. When we reached the area that we were assigned to pick, the land was usually moist from the previous night's dew, and often the furrows in the field were frozen or white with frost. Digging into the frozen—or partially frozen—ground in search of a cluster of potatoes is not a pleasant task. We wore cotton gloves for picking, but these soon became worn, wet, cold, and very uncomfortable.

There was little we could do to ease our discomfort as we picked through the early morning darkness until dark shadows fell in the late afternoon. For this backbreaking work we were paid five cents per barrel, and I never thought it was enough for the agony that I suffered. I often wondered later in life if my chronic back problems were a result of those agonizing days (that I thought would never end) working in a damp potato field.

As much as I enjoyed the summer school vacation, I looked forward to fall, and being back in school with my friends. I also enjoyed the coolness of the fall air. There was real comfort in wearing a warm sweater once the year moved into October.

Baseballs and softballs were stored away, and footballs were brought forth. We had no organized leagues. A group of us young boys in the neighborhood would walk to a small field near the Bangor & Aroostook Railroad station and the American Customs Office in Madawaska, near the entrance into the U.S. from Canada. The lot provided the thrills of a full-sized football field. I imagined myself as the great "Red" Grange, running the full yardage of the field, breaking tackles along the way, and crossing the goal line for another six points and glory. In reality, the distance was probably not more than twenty yards, but at the time it seemed much greater. During these hard-fought games we wore no helmets, no shoulder pads or padded pants, only the clothes that we happened to be wearing. Often, I ended the game with a rip in my shirt or grass stains covering the knees of my pants; I expected to get a scolding from my parents for the wear and tear on my clothing, but I never did.

Another favorite pastime was picking nuts. Not far from where we played football was an area filled with hazelnut trees. In the fall we would pick the hazelnuts by the hour. We were very careful to avoid the green prickly cover that protected the inner shell surrounding the nut, as it was very painful if the sharp burrs pierced the tips of our fingers.

After gathering a sizeable amount of hazelnuts, I would place them very carefully into an empty burlap potato bag and pound the filled bag on a concrete sidewalk or beat it with a heavy rock. This would make the burry green coverings break down, turn brownish, and be more easily removed from the shell of the nut. Once the green cover had been removed, I would put the nut into my mouth, cracking the shell with my back teeth, and chew the luscious meat of the nut. Some nuts were too hard to crack with my teeth, and I got to the meat of those by placing the shell on a flat rock and pounding it open with a stone. The savory taste of the hazelnuts remained with me for days.

In the forested area south of the town, there was another area where I could gather nuts. On the ridge of a hilly area, I found a stand of beech trees, which in the fall dropped nuts onto the ground. I wasn't the only one who came to pick up the fallen nuts. Deer came onto the ridge for the same reason, and on many afternoons I would jump a deer pawing through the leaves for the same treasure I looked for. Beechnuts are not as difficult to open as hazelnuts; the double-diamond-shaped nuts are enclosed in a softer shell that can be opened without difficulty. The smaller nuts are just as enjoyable to eat.

We found other shrubs that supplied us with the season's delicacies. Chokecherries were picked and eaten in such abundance that our mouths would pucker up so we could hardly speak. When we had gathered most of the fruit available in town and on the edge of town, there were other trees that caught our interest. One such tree was the poplar tree. We would cut a branch and tap the bark with the body of a jackknife until the bark softened, which allowed us to slip the bark off the branch. Once removed, we would flatten one end of the branch, and notch this section of the branch about four inches from the end. We would then slide the bark that we had removed back over the branch, leaving us with a whistle that worked as well as any store-bought one. If we lost our whistle, or damaged it by constant use, we simply made another one.

Fall was the season for burning leaves and dried grass. I could rake leaves and dried grass over a fire for hours, watching the smoke billow skyward and suddenly break into a glowing flame, only to be covered again and again, repeated until only a pile of white ashes remained. I watched my father burn grass when I was not allowed to do it myself, and it is one of my favorite memories. I loved the warmth of the fire and the permeating smell of the smoke. It was so wonderful to be outdoors when the chill of the air was counterbalanced by the heat from the pile of burning leaves.

None of my neighborhood friends ever smoked tobacco, but the smell of burning leaves triggered our senses to crumble dry maple leaves and roll them into cigarette paper that we purchased at Gardner's store for a nickel. We'd touch a lighted match to the tip of our self-made cigarettes, always out of sight of our parents. We thought ourselves quite grown-up, as most of the mill workers in town smoked. The dry leaves burned quickly, and one puff was the limit of each cigarette.

Deer hunting season occurred every fall. My father was a hunter, and he enjoyed the excitement of tramping through the woods and searching for the elusive whitetails. He liked to hunt better than any other sport, and would yearn for opening day of the season to arrive each year. If you asked him in June (or any other month) how many days were left until the deer season opened, he could tell you to the day. He would count the days from the end of one season until the next hunting season opened. He couldn't wait until I was old enough to get interested in the sport, and when I turned twelve, he purchased a 410-gauge single-barrel shotgun for me, and I began the first of many years of hunting with him.

When he felt that he had taught me enough about gun safety, he allowed me to hunt on Saturday afternoons by myself. I never hunted for deer in my beginning years as a hunter, but would travel through the wooded area on the edge of town or walk the farm roads along the potato fields searching for partridge. On several occasions I would fire my shotgun at a stump or a clump of bushes, which for some reason looked exactly like a partridge. The sun and shadows could affect what I saw at different times of the day, especially late in the afternoon, and, even though alone, I would feel embarrassed by my mistake. I never told my father about these incidents, as I feared he would have terminated my hunting privileges without further notice.

In later times my father and I discussed the fact that some hunters were accidentally shot during the hunting season, and he agreed with me that lighting and shadows in the woods at the end of the day can play terrible tricks on one's imagination, and what one believes one is shooting. I came to the conclusion after these conversations, although he never admitted it, that he had misfired at stumps and bushes when he first hunted. He taught me well and repeated to me many times over that I should never pull the trigger on any firearm unless I was absolutely sure that I could identify my target.

As an adult I hunted with my father often, and his advice paid off on an afternoon when we were together in the woods. My father had the intention of staying in one specific spot for the entire day. I was to take a position approximately a quarter-mile from him but beyond his scope of vision. I sat on the side of a ridge, which I thought was a good vantage point.

Later in the afternoon, I noticed a motion that I thought was a deer moving in my direction. I stood up, and sighted in on the moving object. I thought I saw the head of a buck bobbing up and down following the scent of a doe. At the time, blaze orange jackets and hats were not required to hunt deer in Maine, and we wore green, which was the customary hunting color at the time. I had my forward and rear sights focused in on the moving object, but what I thought was a deer was still a good distance away. As I watched, I thought of what my father had told me many times—"Don't pull the trigger unless you are absolutely sure of your target."

As the buck advanced closer to my position, my body began to shake, and my heart beat to such a degree that I thought I could hear it. My adrenaline was rising rapidly. Suddenly, I dropped my gun sights down, placed the safety back on, and thought for a moment that I would collapse. I had sighted in on my father. As he came towards me, my mind was filled with thought of what might have been had I pulled the trigger and killed my father. How would I ever have told my mother? How could I have lived with myself? When I thought of the consequences of such an act, it was difficult to hide my shame as my father reached me.

I never told him how close I had come to firing my rifle in his direction. I explained that I was shivering because I was chilled from sitting in the cold of the day for so long without moving. I tried to change the subject to anything but the deer that I thought I had seen.

Silently, I thanked God for preventing me from pulling the trigger. From that day on, I have been a different hunter, and killing a deer is not that important to me. It's the beauty of God's creation in the woods that's important, and I thank Him for that beauty and for protecting my mentor on a day that I could have destroyed his life and mine.

A friend and I had a business venture when I turned thirteen. The houses in my neighborhood were heated with either wood or coal furnaces, with wood as the main heating source. Early in the fall, wood arrived in truckload lots and was dumped along the foundation of each Fraser Company–owned house. There were windows that gave access to the cellars of all these homes. My closest friend in the neighborhood was Stanley Goodell. He and I went to each home and arranged to throw their supply of wood into the cellar, all for a fee of 25 cents per cord. The fee included stacking the wood away from other objects in the basement, allowing the residents easy access to their wood during the fall and winter heating season.

Most of the residents agreed to give us the work, which occupied our time for about six weeks. It was hard work, resulting in bruised fingers and an occasional splinter, but we considered it worth our time. Stanley and I strove for perfection, carefully avoiding furnaces and other objects when we threw the wood into the cellars. After the wood was inside, we piled it neatly in stacks, placing each stick of wood snugly against the next. When finished, the stacks were compact, leaving the owners more space for other storage. Our work was always approved by the owner, after which we would receive our compensation and leave, proud of our high-quality results. Stanley and I would stop a short distance from each home that we finished, and I would say, "Good job, Stan," and he would respond with, "Good job, Ron." We'd smile at each other and walk home.

All of my friends in the neighborhood and I looked forward to Halloween. It was our day of reckoning with some of the neighborhood families who we considered crotchety or insensitive to the ways of young children. A few of our neighbors were on our list. One was always hollering at us to keep off his lawn. Another didn't seem to like anyone in the neighborhood, children or otherwise, and another would growl at us after he'd had a few drinks on pay night. There was no option between "trick or treat" when it came to families we didn't like. They were scheduled to have a trick played on them, and this was planned well in advance of Halloween. The tricks weren't necessarily vicious, but they could be messy if eggs were broken against parlor windows, or if garbage cans were toppled over, strewing a week's garbage all over lawns or driveways. Some tricks could cause some inconvenience to the homeowner as well; for instance, finding that air in their car tires had been let out when they came out in a hurry to go somewhere.

On the Halloween evening when I was thirteen, one of my non-vicious tricks got out of hand. I was walking home, completely satisfied with all our "tricks" and the fun night we had had. As I walked through Mr. Johnson's yard, I noticed a small, two-wheel trailer that was hitched to the back of a car and was used to haul rubbish to the dump. The Johnsons' street was a hilly one, with an incline of about twenty degrees, and I thought it would be great fun to move the trailer out to the street, and then ease it to the bottom of the hill where it would be found the next morning. Knowing that both Mr. and Mrs. Johnson were hard of hearing, I had no problem moving the trailer to the edge of their driveway, undetected by either of them. However, I underestimated the weight of the trailer, and when I turned the trailer into the slope of the hill, I realized that I couldn't restrain the forward movement of it, even though I used the entire strength of my small body to hold it from going forward. The trailer was on its way to the bottom of the hill, and I could do nothing about it. It didn't make it to the bottom of the hill. Parked across the street from where I lived, which was below the Johnson residence, was an automobile owned by someone who happened to be visiting the Gilberts, our neighbors directly across from our house. There was a loud crash as the trailer lodged in the radiator of the parked vehicle.

I ran in the opposite direction from my home as fast as my legs would carry me. After allowing sufficient time for any reaction to occur, I edged myself home. There seemed to be no damage to the trailer, but the vehicle that it had crashed into had sustained considerable damage to its radiator. When I entered my home, I went straight to bed, avoiding any questions that my parents may have had about strange noises occurring earlier in the evening outside our home.

The following morning, I expressed the same surprise others did as they gathered around the damaged vehicle, voicing concerns as to how anyone could perform such a devastating act, and wondering what this younger generation was coming to. I sided with the adult comments, avoided eye-to-eye contact with my father, and was afraid to say anything for fear that he would be made responsible for the damages. I was thankful that he never thought I was capable of such a deed, and he never questioned my involvement.

Many years later I confessed to my father what had happened on that Halloween night. I hadn't lied to him, as he never had asked if I was involved, but I knew that I had been deceitful. I felt much better after I had told. My father made no comment after my confession. I appreciated his silence, which told me that he must have understood how bad and ashamed I had felt at the time the incident happened.

Knowing my father, having heard my confession, he would have contacted the Gilberts, learned whose car had been damaged on that Halloween night, and made some restitution, without ever mentioning it to me.

Chapter Eleven

Family Guidance and Father's Moods

I cannot forget the support that my parents provided throughout my early years. When I had an earache, my mother was there. When I took an interest in golf, my father was there. When I took a fall and skinned my knees, both parents were there. When I needed answers to what I considered a problem, both were there again to help me and provide an answer that I would understand. They had a complete understanding of my needs as a young boy. And yet, they allowed me the freedom to find my own niche in life with few restrictions on my movements while I searched for my own identity. This is not to suggest that I could do as I wished without their guidance or discipline.

Most couples differ in their temperaments, emotions and attitudes. My parents were no exception, but they seemed to understand their differences and lived in support of each other and in support of their only child. They celebrated their fiftieth wedding anniversary in 1970, a testament to their love and commitment to each other.

My father was the disciplinarian. He was also my mentor. He took me aside one evening when I was about ten years old and explained the "birds and the bees," as we referred to sex education in those days. He spent a great deal of time with me on the importance of growing up with principles. Principles were very important to him, and he had a passionate dislike for anyone who lied or cheated in any way. My father had a limited education, having left school after the eighth grade to work on his father's farm. Nonetheless, he was self-educated and possessed good common sense, which I have come to believe carries more importance than a person with a college degree who doesn't know enough "to come in out of the rain." He stressed more than anything else that I should be an honorable person in my association with others. When he questioned me for any reason, he would expect a truthful answer, having assured me that he would never punish me if told the truth.

Fortunately, I was never questioned about the Halloween incident referred to previously, in which my own carelessness caused a car to be damaged. In a way, I violated his trust by not admitting to him that I had been responsible for the accident, but my rationale at the time was to avoid the cost of repairs that I was certain my father would have to pay. Had he questioned me specifically, I would have admitted my guilt, for throughout our lives we shared our problems with each other, and to the best of my knowledge harbored no secrets.

There were times, however, when my father was a very difficult person. He was not a heavy-drinking man, like many other mill workers, but he was troubled by mood swings. Some insignificant incident would bother him and that would spawn explosive fits of anger. The mysterious grudge he held would last for days, during which time he wouldn't speak to my mother or me. We would get the silent treatment until one day he would sheepishly

My mother and I visit Grandfather Stewart's farm in St. George, New Brunswick.

smile and apologize. Then the household would return to normal.

These mood changes came very infrequently, and my mother always defended him with an explanation that these fits of anger were an aftermath of his time in the service during World War I. He had been in the first battalion of Canadians who went overseas in the war, and was involved in all of the major battles in which the Canadians fought. My father survived the battles of Vimy Ridge, the Ypres, and the battle of the Somme. (He didn't know then that the racks of dead soldiers piled in a field where the battle of the Somme had taken place contained the body of Charles Bernard Conway, the nineteen-year-old brother of his yet-unknown future wife. My mother's oldest brother was killed only a few days before the Armistice was signed.)

My mother would also explain that my father's fits of annoyance could be attributed to his near-death struggle in the icy waters of Lake Utopia of New Brunswick in 1919, before they were married. My fearless father and a friend had decided to put their canoe into Lake Utopia, a short distance from St. George, to fish on the 24th of May. This was a Canadian holiday to celebrate Queen Victoria's birthday. (Schoolchildren would say, "The 24th of May is the Queen's birthday; if we don't have a holiday, we'll all run away.")

Upon catching an oversized trout, one of them—either my father or his friend—reacted excitedly and capsized the canoe. They clung to the gunnels of the canoe for the next two and a half hours, in a frigid lake and a chilling breeze, hollering for help to no avail. Neither had the strength to upright the canoe. Then, a miracle happened. Another boat came directly to them without realizing that someone was in trouble, or even seeing them in advance. My father and his friend later learned the boaters had heard their cries but thought they were the cries of loons, which were quite prevalent on the lake. Both my father and his friend had a death grip on the sides of the overturned canoe, and their hands had to be pried loose. The friend never really recovered and spent the greater part of his remaining life in a mental institution. My mother often wondered in later years if my father's mishap on Lake Utopia contributed to his occasional mood swings.

Most of the time he was a docile person, spending much of his time in the living room, listening to the radio or reading. He was an armchair sportsman and could quote statistics on baseball or hockey as well as anyone I ever knew. He loved to play cards and preferred that his card-playing friends come to play at his house. There wasn't much that would lure him from his own home, except deer season in the fall. Hunting was his favorite pastime.

As a result of one of his hunting trips, he expected to be fired from his job with Fraser Paper. He and the mill manager and a dye company salesman from Boston had planned a hunting trip

My mother, Mary, and father, Gordon, celebrate my graduation from the University of Maine in 1949.

near Grand Falls, New Brunswick, and so a Canadian guide was required. The dye salesman wasn't a hunter, but he enjoyed the camaraderie of men in a hunting camp, and he especially enjoyed the company of my father, as they had been friends for years.

While my father and his friend were taking an afternoon snooze, the mill manager removed some money from the friend's wallet, according to the Canadian guide who saw what happened and told my father later. My father suppressed his anger until that evening, and over a few drinks, confronted the mill manager about the theft. The manager admitted to taking the money as a prank, and said he intended to return it. My father thought otherwise and blackened both of his boss's eyes, requiring him to remain in Canada an extra week until the swelling went down and the coloring paled.

My father fully expected to lose his job, but the incident was never mentioned again. However, my father's friendship with the manager was lost forever. There was no gray area with my father—if he liked you, he would give you the shirt off his back, but if he didn't, he would mince no words, so much so that at times, he embarrassed me by his frankness.

Except for times when I brought on the need for disciplinary action, my association with my father was always good. In addition to golf, we often would play cribbage by the hour. My mother joined us for a card game called "nines," a form of three-handed bridge. The fall season always brought about the anticipation of hunting together, and as that ended, the hockey season started. We attended as many hockey games as we could.

Speaking of bringing about disciplinary action upon myself, there was one particular time when I really came under my father's wrath. I was sixteen, beginning to notice girls, and learning to dance with them. My friends and I used to frequent a small dance hall and ice cream parlor in Frenchville, about eight miles up the St. John River from Madawaska. When one of us could get a parent's car, we had no problem getting there, but as the government began rationing gas, family cars were not available to most of us, so we needed another means of transportation.

My father, Gordon H. Stewart, with our black-and-tan coonhound, Smokey.

We had discovered that the Bangor and Aroostook Railroad left unlocked handcars beside the tracks, and it was an easy task for three or four of us boys to lift the car onto the tracks and pump our way back and forth to Frenchville. None of the freight trains in that section of the state ever ran at night, so we saw no apparent danger or harm in borrowing the handcars for a few hours. Unbeknownst to us, however, the Bangor and Aroostook Railroad had been experiencing thefts from the freight cars left on the tracks. The war had recently started in Europe, and we were further unaware that the Fraser Paper Company had recently hired armed guards to patrol their property adjacent to the B & A rails.

On the particular night that excited my father's wrath, Stanley Goodell, Billy King and I had just placed a handcar on the tracks when we were confronted with a voice saying, "Halt and put your hands into the air!" Billy froze, but Stanley and I jumped down the embankment away from the mill and toward the St. John River, which ran parallel with the B & A tracks.

Once Stanley and I had reached the riverbank, we walked back up into town. We were standing at the top of Bridge Street when my father came along, having been to Bill Parent's Drugstore to pick up a copy of the *Bangor Daily News*. At the same time, the town's single police cruiser was racing down Bridge Street to the mill. My father inquired as to what was going on. Stanley and I wondered the same thing. We didn't know that Billy was now being held by the mill's armed guard. Billy, frightened by the guard's questions, admitted that he had not acted alone and revealed that Stanley and I had been his accomplices. Billy was immediately arrested and placed in the local jail.

Meanwhile, another friend, Don McDermott, came by with his father's car and picked us up and drove us to Edmundston. When we returned to Madawaska, the police chief was waiting at the customshouse and asked Stanley and I to get out of Don's car, which we did with trepidation. The chief questioned us, but for some reason did not arrest us.

At home, Mrs. King was raging with anger that she had to post a bail bond to release Billy from jail. She came to my house and asked my father to drive her to Van Buren, about thirty miles southeast of Madawaska, where the bail bond had to be issued by Judge McManus. Since neither Stanley's nor Billy's father owned a car, my father agreed to do what Mrs. King had asked, and took Stanley and me with him.

I failed to note in describing my father thus far that he found it difficult to say three words without two of them being "cuss" words. My mother defended him on that bad habit as well, claiming that he never took God's name in vain until he started working in the woods at Estcourt, Quebec, on his first job with the Fraser Company. I heard all of his swear words that evening.

On our way home from Van Buren, my father's limited amount of gasoline ran dry in St. David, and we had to walk the last four miles home. Stanley and I were subjected to a verbal tirade from my father over the last four miles, a tongue-lashing that I never forgot. It was well deserved and we accepted it in silence.

CHAPTER TWELVE

My Mother, the Family Peacemaker

As vociferous as my father was on occasions, my mother was the opposite. I seldom saw my mother angry, and throughout her life she was our family's peacemaker. She had a way of calming my father when he was in one of his moods, and when I grew older and faced the tensions of raising a family, she often calmed my moods as well. I'm sure many people feel about their mothers the way that I felt about mine; she was the most understanding woman that I have ever known. Like many women, she loved to talk, but never did I hear her say anything disparaging about another person. She listened to rumors with disbelief and often was very defensive against anyone who criticized another in her presence.

Although she was raised in a Catholic family and attended parochial schools, she was not considered to be a member of the Catholic Church because she had married my father, a Baptist. Still, she said her rosary faithfully each night and never stopped believing in Catholicism. She communicated to me a strong sense of religion, even though I did not attend church as a small boy. Because of her influence, I have never, as a youngster and to this day, taken God's name in vain. My father may have influenced me against swearing as well, since he cussed enough for both of us.

My mother's difficulties with pregnancy meant that I ended up being an only child. My early life, as a result, was without want and she doted on me in every way. Still, I never felt pampered; I had the love of both my mother and father and believed it was only natural that they shared a lot of their time with me.

It was my mother who comforted me and attended to me when I became ill. It seemed that I was subjected to every virus that came along and contracted the flu more often than most, with escalating body temperatures and high fevers that would keep me in bed for three and four days at a time. I didn't escape catching measles and chicken pox, and was constantly bothered by earaches, which were usually alleviated a great deal by my mother blowing cigarette smoke in my ear when the pain became severe. The strange part is that my mother never smoked, and would cough constantly and wrinkle her face in disgust while using one of my father's cigarettes. She would repeat this remedy on many evenings when my earaches became unbearable and I cried for her comforting ways.

As noted earlier, my mother was a shopper, a sickness she passed on to me. As hard as I try, I am very much a compulsive buyer, and even today I can't resist a bargain, whether I need the item or not. Throughout her married life, my mother had an afternoon ritual, that involved walking uptown and visiting J.J. Newberry, the first store she came to on her walk. She would then go into Ozithe Daigle's Department Store for Women and converse with Ozithe. Her next stop would be Rice's Furniture store, as she loved to look at furniture and imagine what piece would fit where in our home. She would end her daily tour by picking up the local newspaper at Bill Parent's Rexall Drug.

She checked prices daily, and when she found a "steal," she was hooked and bought the item whether she needed it or not. Table lamps were a particular weakness of hers, and Ambrose Marquis, who managed the J.J. Newberry store, once asked me what my mother ever did with all the lamps she bought. He explained to me that all he had to do to sell a lamp to my mother was to drop the price. It was embarrassing for me to tell Ambrose that most of the lamps that she carted home were in use, with some of the end tables in our house having more than one lamp on them. She thought they were pretty, so why not have two lamps on the same table?

There were other times when she came across a bargain and didn't have the money to buy it. In that case, she would protect her find by asking the merchant to put it away for her. She would then pay on it each week until it was paid for, and only then would she bring it home. I think this was the same as department store layaway plans. Credit cards were not in existence in those days, and I doubt if many stores had a layaway plan, but she had her own ways of getting something she liked and wanted.

Occasionally, she would take me uptown, and I must admit that I enjoyed shopping with her, as she always made some small purchase for me, even though it was not my habit to ask for anything. As a result of these shopping sprees, I became a collector in my own right, searching constantly for Big Little Books, comic books or postage stamps, the latter remaining my hobby throughout my adult life. There were no stores that sold postage stamps for collectors in Madawaska, so I picked up this hobby when I shopped with her in Saint John, New Brunswick. The British Empire covered much of the world in the '30s, and the stamps of

England with its many colonies were sold in packets in the various cigar stores and small shops on King Street and Charlotte Street in the city. The stamps always pictured the royal family in pretentious raiment, which provided the stamps with much color. Having bought my first packet of stamps and gazing at them with much enjoyment, I never imagined at that point that I would become, as I am still, a philatelist. One of my more memorable Christmas gifts from my parents was the complete coronation issue of Queen Elizabeth and George the Sixth of 1937. This set comprises 202 mint stamps and remains a valued and sentimental part of my collection today.

Big Little Books were the rage when I was a youngster, and I became a collector of them as well. The books were approximately four and one-half inches tall, three and one-half inches wide and two inches thick. I believe that most of the Big Little Books were published by the Whitman Publishing Company in Racine, Wisconsin, at least most of mine were. There were many titles to these books and some of my favorites were: *King of the Royal Mounted*; *Don Winslow, U.S. Navy*; *Terry and the Pirates*; *The Adventures of Tarzan*; *Buck Rogers and the Doomed Comet*; *Dick Tracy and the Boris Arson Gang*; *Alley Oop and Dinny in the Land of Moo*; *Chester Gump in the Land of Gold*; and *Joe Palooka, Boxing Champ*.

These books provided me with a great variety of reading and viewing pleasure, as each written page was accompanied by an opposite page with a related illustration. I used to compete with a neighborhood girl, Betty Beaulier, who also collected them. We had much in common, since she was also an only child whose mother was a fellow shopper and one of my mother's closest friends. Often the two women shopped together and would check the section of the store where the Big Little Books were displayed, both looking for new titles that Betty and I wanted. We always knew when new titles were out, as the publisher listed them on the back pages of the book we had just purchased. Often, however, the store got only one of a certain book, and it was disheartening to find that Betty's mother had made the purchase first and I had missed out. I'm sure that Betty felt the same way when the situation was reversed. Our collecting created competition among our mothers as well, but it never created any loss of friendship, as I'm sure they worked out some sort of rotation system with Betty and I being none the wiser.

It is difficult for me to recall any bad moments between my mother and me during my preteen years. I'm sure that my mother must have had some difficult times with me, but nothing comes to my mind as such. It was the time in my life that play, above everything else, kept me active and relatively healthy. It was a time of new discoveries and daily fantasies. It was a time of bonding between my mother and father and me. They were always there for me but never restrictive, and it was the most insulated time in my life.

Chapter Thirteen

French Family Influence

My childhood friends and I were from different backgrounds, brought together by our respective parents who came to the Land of the Porcupine because of the paper mill. English-speaking families were in the minority, and while this fact may have created a problem for our parents, it never surfaced.

Madawaska was inhabited by a majority of French-speaking families. The French, who had migrated from an earlier colony of Acadians in Nova Scotia, were hardworking, fun-loving families who faithfully attended the St. Thomas Aquinas Parish Church and twice annually offered a full day's pay as an additional tithing to their weekly offering. There was no Protestant church in Madawaska, and although there were two in Edmundston, they were beyond a reasonable walking distance, so my earlier teachings and association with a church was somewhat limited.

The religious and language differences between me and most of my childhood playmates were never a factor in our ability to play and have fun together. Somehow, we communicated; however, it was quite noticeable that the French children were more adaptable to learning the English language than the English were in learning French.

Religion was never discussed, although as I grew older, I became more aware that many French families were averse to my dating their daughters. It was considered a cardinal sin for a Catholic to marry someone outside of the faith, even though at our ages, marriage was far from our thoughts.

I admired most of the French people I knew. They had large families who cared for each other and cared for others as well. I remember they loved to dance and gather around a fiddle-playing family member and sing songs in both French and English.

I recall the Martin family, who at one time owned a woolen mill in Madawaska. They were one of the few families not employed by the Fraser Paper Company. They were independent, industrious, and carefree. Their woolen mill became one of my favorite haunts. One of their sons was a playmate of mine. His family called him "Ti Blue," although I never knew why. Ti Blue would invite me to his house, and we were allowed to run through the mill and jump into the wool that had been recently spun on antiquated machinery running on its last legs. Ti Blue had many siblings, and after we finished playing and were covered with lint from the wool, I was always invited into their home, where I would be brushed off and served cookies and milk. (Unfortunately, shortly after being introduced to this wonderful play area, the mill went out of business.)

In later years, Ti Blue became a commercial artist and did very well in southern Maine. His brother, Pat, became a good friend, who would often visit and bring along his fiddle, playing for my wife and me. A sister, Mary May—who must have been born with a smile on her face, for she was always so pleasant and "full of it"—also remained a friend in later years. She, like myself, became politically active in the local affairs of Madawaska.

I feel so fortunate that I knew so many families like the Martins when I was in my early years. Their industrious and light-hearted ways touched my life and helped to develop many of my own positive characteristics that I would not have otherwise acquired.

CHAPTER FOURTEEN

Madawaska Pay Nights

Madawaska was a mill town, and some of the papermakers were heavy drinkers. The mill paid their workers on Thursday, and for the next three nights it was party time. We always knew when it was midnight on Thursday, for we had one neighbor who never failed to close the local pub every pay night and then announce his journey home by singing Irish ballads as loud as he could. My mother, who always stayed up late, would say to herself, "There goes Tommy; it must be time for me to turn in."

Tommy was harmless, but he was huge. Even though he had his weekly "toot" on payday, he always went home and showed much affection for his wife and family. He was always buying gifts for his children, who I know were embarrassed by their father's weekly drunkenness.

One Fourth of July, Tommy purchased a large supply of fireworks. He carefully prepared his display so that when the first fuse was lit, it would lead to the second one, and so on, lighting the entire display in a short time to its full glow. The display was set up on his front porch, and he had cautioned everyone not to come onto the porch, or to strike a match anywhere in the vicinity. It was very important that no one got careless, he explained.

Tommy was working the midnight to eight a.m. shift on that particular Fourth of July weekend. He apparently decided to visit the local pub for a quick one before going home. One quick one led to three or four more drinks, and when he got home by midday, he was staggering. As he stumbled up the stairs of his front porch, he pulled out a cigarette and lit up. By accident, Tommy's cigarette touched one of the fuses he had cautioned everyone else not to approach. In seconds the entire porch was aglow with Roman candles bursting out in the direction of the street, spinning wheels spinning and firecrackers bursting in loud reports, breaking the silence of an otherwise peaceful afternoon. Tommy stood there blissfully, puffing on his cigarette, amidst the path of whizzing pyrotechnics. My friends and I gaped with amazement at what would have been a sensational display of fireworks, if the sun had only set.

Some of our other neighbors, also in the habit of getting inebriated at least one night of the week, were not as easygoing as Tommy. One neighbor, whom I shall call Henry, became quite belligerent after spending a few hours in one of the local bars.

Henry's wife boarded two young, unmarried mill workers, who learned to stay clear of Henry when he had been drinking. In fact, they were quite frightened of him when he had been imbibing. One summer evening, however, there was no escaping Henry, who had already consumed more alcohol than he should have, and was heading home with only one thought on his mind—to throw the two boarders out of his house. Before Henry could even roll up his sleeves, the two boarders were on their way to the local hotel.

With no one left in the house to direct his anger toward, he grabbed his pet parrot and threw him out onto the street. Not satisfied with that, Henry loaded up his shotgun and fired at the parrot as it flew from one telephone wire to the next. Fortunately for the parrot, Henry was probably seeing more than one target. He missed on two or three attempts, and the parrot escaped without harm.

Again, my friends and I witnessed this display of uncontrolled anger with the same kind of amazement as when we watched Tommy's unscheduled fireworks presentation. The only difference was that we crouched below the banking of an adjacent lawn until Henry reentered his house. The parrot took cover as well, and disappeared for the entire night. The next morning Henry's wife asked the neighborhood children to go looking for her "Polly." Polly was located, and to the best of my knowledge, lived out the remaining years of his life peacefully.

However, as far as I was concerned, I would have been just as pleased if we had never found that parrot. When my mother wanted me to come home, she would stand on our front doorstep and yell, "RONALD!" Henry and his wife lived next door to us, and the parrot learned to imitate my mother. Very often I would hear "RONALD!" and it was impossible for me to distinguish whether it was Polly or my mother. As a result, I was constantly running home unnecessarily, and at times I wanted to ask for Henry's shotgun and shoot the parrot myself!

Chapter Fifteen

Teenager, 1938

When I became a teenager, the year was 1938. Tensions in international politics were escalating. Although I never really understood how serious the problem was becoming in Europe, Adolf Hitler's name was on everyone's lips. In Germany, he was considered a messiah by many, and his many followers were proof of that; but to surrounding countries, and especially to England, he became a threat to world peace.

I can recall vividly the day that England declared war on Germany. It was the Labor Day weekend of 1939. My parents and I were traveling to New Brunswick for the weekend. My father stopped in Houlton about noontime to pick up a copy of the *Bangor Daily News*, which headlined the commencement of World War II. I can remember my father's words of assurance that I had nothing to fear, and that it would all be over by the time I became of age to serve. How wrong he was!

What is even more vivid in my memories of that year is an event that occurred a few days after the visit with my grandparents. As I prepared to enter school for another year, my parents were advised by the U.S. Customs Service that once I crossed the border into Edmundston, I would not be allowed to reenter the United States. At that point in time, evidently due to newly escalating tensions, I was considered to be an alien of the United States. Both of my parents had been naturalized as U.S. citizens in the mid-'30s, but I had planned to continue with a dual citizenship status until I reached twenty-one. It took nearly four weeks before proper documentation was completed, allowing me to return to my school and studies in Canada.

School life seemed little affected by the war in Europe, although it became noticeable that older boys in town were fast disappearing from the usual haunts. Many of them were coming home to visit in uniform, and little did they know that many were home for the last time.

As teenagers, we carried on without fully understanding the atrocities of war. We were reminded of the war through the headlines in the *Bangor Daily News* or the *Saint John Telegraph Journal*, and on the weekly Pathe newsreels that preceded our Saturday afternoon movies. Major news reports coming out of Europe became matters of discussion during schoolyard recesses, or when we sat over Cokes and fries at the local hangout.

Stories of the British fleet caused the most excitement. We followed the reports that the British had cornered the German battleship, the *Bismarck*, in a Norwegian fjord, with later reports that the Germans themselves had scuttled the pride of Hitler's fleet. We were excited again when word was received that another German battleship had also been scuttled in the South Atlantic. In less than six years, I would be serving on a ship that would anchor in Montevideo, Uruguay, and I would view firsthand the mast of the mighty *Graf Spee*, as it protruded from the waters of Montevideo harbor—as the only remaining monument to a ship that had brought fear to many who had served with the Allied forces.

The British, however, were not without their losses, and we were greatly saddened when the HMS *Hood* was sunk.

Many of the French families in the St. John Valley were related to each other, either closely or distantly, and as depressed as some students became because of losses due to the war, there was a camaraderie that retained a spark of joy and happiness even through the darkest of times. My friends and I developed a sense of patriotism that was heightened by the movies being shown at the Star Theatre. Although we were soon to be young men, our innocence then made us unaware that the film industry, through its subtle propaganda that we witnessed every Saturday afternoon, was influencing our willingness to be caught up in the war effort.

I began to feel stirrings to join the navy, but even stronger urges won out, and I put my focus on girlfriends, dance parties and the music of the big bands.

Chapter Sixteen

Humor Offsets World Concerns

My teenage years passed quickly. My graduation day in June of 1942 was approaching. The war in Europe had escalated, and even though we were far removed from the war, signs of that terrible time in our history were becoming noticeable.

Many of the boys who had graduated before me joined the war effort upon leaving high school. My classmate, John Scott, had already lost two older brothers after they had enlisted in the Royal Canadian Air Force. One brother, Philip, had been shot down over Malta, and the other, Keith, had been killed in a takeoff accident in England. It was a terrible time for John, and even more so for Mrs. Scott, whose hair had turned pure white, according to the rumors that had come back to our school. John also enlisted upon graduation, without the approval of his mother, and within a year experienced the same fate as his brothers. He was shot down over Germany and did not survive. Mrs. Scott never fully recovered from losing three of her four sons in the war.

For every action, there is a reaction. My reaction to the gloom that seemed to permeate all of our young lives at that time was to search for humor. Even though at times it was difficult, humor became an important part of my daily thoughts, providing me with an escape from the tragic stories that were told over and over and became more frequent as the war escalated. I tried to capture every piece of humor that was offered. I became a faithful listener of *The Bob Hope Show*, repeating his one-liners in the schoolyard the following morning to whomever would listen.

Teachers also recognized that the daily war reports were beginning to depress many students. They eased up on us a little and offered us stories of their own. Even though I can't recall jokes that I have heard in the past week, I remember the first real joke that I ever heard from an adult, my French teacher, Rene Fournier. Mr. Fournier always claimed that he was half French and half Irish, with his Irish half being the part that he sat on. His story starts with a woman boarding a Pullman sleeping car. She had been assigned a top berth on the passenger train, and immediately climbed up into it and made herself comfortable. The berth beneath her was assigned to a gentleman, unknown to her. Throughout the day, the poor woman developed a condition of flatulence. Once settled in her bunk, she continued to break wind, causing the air within her sleeping area to become quite odorous. The man who occupied the berth below her soon noted her problem. In need of fresh air, he opened the window of his berth, stuck his head out, and breathed in. The woman above could no longer stand the same odorous conditions in her confined space, opened her window, and stuck her head out as well. When she did, she looked downward and noted that the man below her was looking up. She didn't know quite what to say and, embarrassed, asked, "By chance do you have the evening paper?"

The man replied, "No, but I'll try to grab a handful of leaves on the next turn."

In the final two years of high school, my friends became more important to me. We shared our feelings about what the future would have in store for us. Would the war in Europe be over and if so, when? We felt many of the same anxieties, concerns, and fears as we approached our last days as schoolchildren.

My closest friend during these days was a fellow student of my age whose name was Vance Toner. We were both short, standing five foot six, although Vance always claimed that he was taller than me. We became inseparable in the last two years of high school; whenever you saw Vance, you were likely to see me, and vice versa. We both loved music and aspired to be songwriters, although we never wrote or composed anything original; but instead, we would alter the lyrics of well-known songs. We made many changes, but only one recollection comes to me after so many years out of high school. Having watched *The Bob Hope Show* weekly, we became familiar with his theme song, "Thanks for the Memory." I suggested to Vance that we change the words to represent our feelings toward the enemies that we were fighting in Europe. We wrote the following to that tune:

Thanks for the memory
Of U-boat 29
Going up the Rhine
With Hitler and his fishes
Washing dirty dishes
Oh, thank you so much.

Thanks for the memory
Of Mussolini, the "wop"
Spinning like a top
And hanging from a tree
For all allies to see
Oh, thank you so much.

Pretty sad, as I look back. Our aspirations to becoming songwriters never materialized. I believe the reason is quite clear.

Vance and I had parts in the only school play (to my knowledge) that Edmundston High ever presented. It wasn't my participation in the play that I remember. It was what happened before the play had its opening night. During one of the rehearsal evenings, the school's night janitor caught me kissing Rachel Matheson, who also had a part in the play. I had kissed her many times before, so it was not a new experience for me. What happened next, however, was.

We were both called into the principal's office the next morning. We were severely lectured about our conduct at school and threatened with dismissal. Graduation was approaching, and the threat really concerned me. I couldn't understand why the principal was coming down so hard on me and not also blaming Rachel for her part in the kiss.

Most (if not all) of our relationships with our female classmates were honorable. We kissed at parties, but that was as intimate as we got. None of us was ever serious with any particular girl, and we traveled together in groups as friends, not as promiscuous beings. We spent a lot of time together at each others' homes and were always welcomed by parents at whichever home we selected for our weekend gatherings. We might have had a particular preference for one of the girls in the group, and vice versa, but it wasn't particularly noticeable. We played records by Glen Miller, Tommy Dorsey, Louis Prima, and others, and interchanged dancing partners throughout the evening. We would stop occasionally—not for a cigarette, as none of us smoked—but possibly to smooch a little and have a Coca-Cola. When it was time to go, a parent would remind us, and we'd go. We would walk home as a group, singing and talking loudly and extending our wonderful evening to the eleventh hour. We'd make sure the girls got home safely, even though there was little fear that they would run into any problem on our safe streets. In the winter, when we didn't meet at a friend's house, we gathered at a restaurant in the Royal Hotel in Edmundston. We would occupy one and often two booths for hours, munching on French fries loaded with salt and covered with ketchup. I now wonder why the management of the restaurant was so tolerant of our presence, as we lingered so long and purchased so little. It must have been a gift of kindness, thinking that otherwise, our gatherings would have been on the streets many nights when the temperature dropped well below zero.

The Edmundston Arena, next to the high school, was another of our favorite meeting places on winter Saturday nights. The enclosed rink was used for high school hockey games from early morning until late in the afternoon. Every boy wanted to play hockey as much as I did, and many weekend mornings we would get up at five A.M. and walk a mile to the rink to play hockey at seven A.M. The arena provided hockey programs for all ages and levels of experience. Evenings were reserved for hockey games between the local Edmundston Eskimos and other teams in the Maritime Hockey League, which included the Moncton Black Hawks, the St. John Beavers and the Halifax Wolverines. Occasionally, the Eskimos would play exhibition games with the

Montreal Canadiens or the Montreal Maroons, both being National Hockey League teams.

On the odd Saturday night when there were no hockey games scheduled, the management of the arena would schedule what were called "moccasin dances," which were a great deal of fun and provided an evening of full delight. The ice surface became our dance floor. To make things romantic, the overhead lights would be dimmed and the ice surface would be illuminated with a colored beam of light shining through a make-believe moon hanging at one end of the rink.

Unfortunately, these effects were wasted on many of us. Dancing in the privacy of a home was one thing, but dancing in public caused many of us to become shy and awkward when it came to asking a girl to dance. Many of the girls at these Saturday night outings were not from our regular groups of friends. Nevertheless, before the dance ended, we would usually summon enough courage to ask a girl to dance, whether we knew her or not. Once on the ice, we would slide across the surface in our gum rubbers, or whatever kind of boots we wore in the winter to keep our feet warm. If we happened to step on our dancing partner's feet, we could place the blame on the size of our boots.

CHAPTER SEVENTEEN

Facing Discrimination

As a schoolboy, I never considered that adults could ever be anything but impartial or fair in their relationships with me. I regarded my parents with respect and I equally respected other adults as well. I was treated fairly by everyone and especially by my teachers from the first grade until my last days of high school graduation. In the days before graduation, I felt discriminated against for the first time. It was very confusing to me.

Throughout all my school years, I was interested in learning and faithfully completed my homework assignments. I studied willingly for tests and final exams. As a result, I was ranked first in my class each year. My ranking didn't necessarily mean that I was the brightest student, but I was diligent in my study habits and got a lot of support from my parents, who realized the importance of education for my life beyond home even though neither of them had completed high school.

My academic accomplishments should have been recognized at the time of my graduation. It never happened. I was disqualified as valedictorian because I was a resident of the United States. The school board had decided that a student living in Canada should have the honor of being valedictorian. My parents and I thought differently. I was still considered by law to be Canadian. After all, I was Canadian-born and held a dual citizenship at that time. My father had served as a Canadian soldier.

To add salt to the wound, I was given no role to play on what should have been a memorable day for me. My name appeared in small print in the graduation program, lost in the list of graduates, and that was it. My thoughts flashed back to my visit to the principal's office a month earlier after being caught kissing Rachel Matheson. The principal had singled me out and threatened to expel me. I thought his suggestion for punishment was a bit excessive, since I had only reported to the principal's office once before, for talking in class in the first grade! He had treated Rachel quite differently and made no mention of punishment to her in any way. Having never been expelled as the principal had threatened earlier, I realized that he was expelling me now at my graduation by disallowing me to be the class valedictorian, an honor which I had earned and deserved.

My mother, normally quiet and always composed, was furious when she learned about the plans for graduation day and that I was not included. She lashed out with an inner fury that I had never witnessed before nor since. She told the principal that the entire school staff and community had insulted me and that she would not allow me to attend the graduation ceremony.

And I didn't. My father suggested that we play golf on that day and forget the entire matter. I was pleased with this suggestion and had a great time with him. It gave me a chance to try out my graduation gift from my parents, a new set of Kenneth Smith golf clubs custom-made for my height and swing. In time, by using the clubs, my game was greatly improved.

For some time after, I pondered who had felt so strongly against me to influence the school board to abort the recognition that should have rightfully been mine on graduation day. As it turned out, I played eighteen holes of golf with my father and was spared the discomfort of sitting in a crowded auditorium on a hot, humid June evening listening to a program that I had lost interest in days before.

Chapter Eighteen

Working in the Mill

The school system in Canada then required only eleven years of study. There was no kindergarten, and there was no twelfth grade, and when I graduated, I had just celebrated my seventeenth birthday. I had another year before I would be subject to the draft for the armed services. It appeared in the summer of 1942 that the war would continue for at least another year. Japan had attacked Pearl Harbor only six months previously.

It was apparent on that infamous day in December of 1941 that my father's prediction that the war would be over before I became of age was not going to hold true. I was listening to the radio on the morning of December 7 when the program was interrupted and President Franklin D. Roosevelt announced that we had been attacked and were at war with Japan. I ran to the kitchen to tell my mother, and she very quickly called my father downstairs. We all sat around our Atwater Kent, listening intently, wondering what the future would bring. Both my parents were troubled by the news and realized that I could soon be called to war. We lived in hope that the United States would quickly strike back, and that the year ahead would bring an armistice.

Most of the boys a year older than me were already in the service, so it was not difficult for me to get a job in the summer of 1942 with the Fraser Company. I was employed as a fifth hand on a paper machine, making about $24 for forty-four hours of work each week. It wasn't an easy job; there was a lot of lifting. The rolls of paper that came off the machines each had a shaft running through them that had to be removed before the rolls, cut in different widths, could be weighed. They were then partially wrapped and moved into the shipping room, where they were examined, wrapped completely, marked and made ready for shipment.

One of Fraser Paper's principal products at the time was paper for drinking straws, through which we sipped our favorite milk shakes and soft drinks. When the mill was making this paper, the fifth hand (me at the time) had little time to rest during an eight-hour shift. The rolls were smaller, with a narrow width, and that meant more shafts to remove and a lot more pushing, weighing, wrapping, and marking.

I also rotated on three shifts of work, which created sleeping problems for me. I never could rest well after working the midnight shift, which commenced at midnight and ended at eight o'clock in the morning. Sleeping during the daylight hours was not easy for me. The midnight shift had its advantages, however, as it was always cooler and workers could take longer rest periods as few of the top management were ever around during those hours. I loved to go out on the mill platform on my break and feel the coolness of the evening and listen to the nighthawks break the quiet of the summer night.

My mother would make me tomato sandwiches, mixed well with mayonnaise and covered heavily with pepper, topped with a thin slice of cheese. How much I enjoyed the flavor of those simple sandwiches.

The thought of leaving home was on my mind constantly as the summer wound down. Soon I would be off to Orono to attend the University of Maine. My father must have been thinking a lot about me leaving home as well, because he played a lot of golf with me that summer. My mother refrained from saying much about my leaving, but I knew that she was worried about what the future held in store for me.

Chapter Nineteen

College and Navy Enlistment

The summer of 1942 passed more quickly than my parents wanted. When September came, they drove me to Orono and dropped me off near the campus bookstore. Watching them drive away, I was very much alone.

I was assigned to a room in a large well-kept Hamlin Street home owned by Hattie Berube and her daughter, Pauline. My living quarters were excellent for a boy who missed his parents. Both women were a delight and treated my two roommates and me as if they had known us for years.

My roommates and I shared a study room and a bedroom on the second floor, which was a new experience for me, never having had a brother or sister to share anything with. I adjusted quickly. John Shurtleff of Jackman, Maine, was very much like myself and loved outdoor sports, so we had much in common. We would trade stories, sometimes well into the night. Freddie Harrison from Bryn Mawr, Pennsylvania, had grown up in a different environment. He was the quiet type and very studious. He spent a great deal of his time listening to John's and my wild and sometimes exaggerated stories about the Maine woods and our girlfriends.

Once on campus, I met other fellows from Aroostook County, and about halfway through my freshman year I was invited to join Phi Eta Kappa, a local fraternity made up mostly of boys from the County. I accepted and made arrangements to move into the fraternity house. Leaving the Berube household and my first friends at the university was a tough decision, but I felt honored to be selected.

In the spring of 1943, "hell week" began on the University of Maine campus. I immediately knew that my normal life would be severely interrupted. John Whitten, a big man on campus, was the president of Phi Eta Kappa. He was the chief assailant of the new pledges to the fraternity, and in a very short time after hell week began, all pledges became members of "Whitten's Fire Brigade." John would take his position at the top of the stairway leading down from the second-floor hallway to the hallway on the first floor. One of his "lieutenants" would instruct me and the other freshman pledges who were assembled in the oversized washroom off the second-floor hallway to fill our mouths with water at the drinking fountain; proceed down the hallway on our hands and knees; go down the stairs to the first-floor hallway and make a sharp right into the living room. We were then to continue on our hands and knees across the living room rug and stop in front of the living room fireplace, where we would spew our mouthful of water onto the blazing fire that glowed brilliantly in front of us. However, before we descended to the first floor, we had to pass "Whitten's Corner," where John swung a mean paddle across our derrieres and literally lifted us over the first three steps to the landing of the stairway that connected the two floors.

Much of the hazing wasn't as threatening as Whitten's Corner, and many of the pledges found humor in some of the exercises. One of the funniest events occurred in the cellar kitchen area of the fraternity house, which became known as the "bombing range."

A large block of ice was set at one end of the large kitchen and a big upright wastebasket was set at the other end. The pledges were asked to disrobe and stand naked in front of the upperclassmen, awaiting our next set of instructions. We then noticed a single shriveled-up grape had been placed on the center of the block of ice. We were told that the grape represented a bomb, and as bombardiers it was our duty to carry the bomb from the point of take-off (the ice block) and drop it over the enemy's headquarters (the waste basket). But we couldn't use our hands. Each of us, in turn, had to position ourselves over the block of ice, somehow maneuver the grape into the crack of our respective asses, and hold it in that position as we waddled across the entire length of the kitchen floor. Then we had to position ourselves over the wastebasket and release our bomb on target, as we yelled, "Bombs away!"

One of our pledges was an enormous young man with an oversized bottom. He was selected to carry the smallest grape that the upperclassmen could find. None of us could contain our laughter as we watched him try to maintain control of the grape as he squeezed his buttocks tightly, waddling across the kitchen floor, making verbal sounds of frustration but reaching his target and releasing his bomb as his fellow pledges hollered praise and clapped their hands. For doing so, all of the pledges had to "resume the position" as Whitten swung his paddle across each of our bare asses. The enjoyment of witnessing that oversized pledge's walk was worth the paddling.

There were a variety of other hell week activities. We were awakened in the middle of the night and asked to eat half a raw onion. We were blindfolded and asked to open our mouths, and then someone would clear their throat loudly and a raw oyster was quickly dropped onto our tongues. That sickened us, causing us to gag and spew out the oyster. We were also taken for a ride after dark and let out about a mile from the fraternity house with instructions to get back to the frat house within the hour.

After hell week our lives returned to normal, and a bond evolved between those who had suffered at the hands of the upperclassmen in our new living quarters. Unfortunately, our friendships were short-lived as each of us became eligible to serve in the armed forces.

In June of 1943, I turned eighteen, and my desire was to join the U.S. Navy and avoid the draft. I hitched a ride to Portland in May and enlisted. (When I was examined by the navy medical officer, he asked me about the black-and-blue marks that remained across my buttocks. I told the officer that a fellow by the name of John Whitten had placed them there during hell week.)

As soon as my enlistment was secured, I called home and told my parents. I knew that my father would understand because he had enlisted in World War I at the same age. I knew it would upset him somewhat to think I'd be soon going to war, but I heard the pride in his voice when I told him that I wanted to be part of the war effort. I also apologized for joining the navy and not the army as he had done. I explained to him that I had nothing against the army, but that during my boyhood trips to Saint John every summer I had been inspired by the Royal Canadian Navy.

My mother, on the other hand, was not pleased. The news of my enlistment upset her terribly, and she quietly wept into the phone. I explained my reasons, but it did little to ease her mind.

Shortly after that phone call to my parents, I was at boot camp in Newport, Rhode Island. I never got off the base in the two months that I was there because we were not allowed liberty until we had learned how to swim. I didn't learn. Daily, they would throw me into the pool, and I would immediately sink to the bottom and wait for a pole to be lowered. I would grab the pole and be pulled to the surface, where they would lift me out and throw me back in. This was repeated again and again. I left Newport after two months of training without any ability to challenge Johnny Weissmuller.

I was given a three-day pass after completing basic training and was assigned to the Fleet Sound School in Key West, Florida. Three days didn't allow me enough time to go home, so my parents came to Boston and stayed at the Parker House, one of the prominent hotels at that time, and I joined them there for a short, emotional visit that meant so much to me. It was an emotional two days. My father apologized to me for any wrongdoing that he had ever inflicted on me. He was concerned that he had spanked me at times, but I knew that when I did get spanked, I had earned it. I had never felt abused by my father or my mother or felt that I had been punished unnecessarily. However, he harbored some guilt about it and with great emotion expressed his love for me. My mother expressed her love as well, but I'll never forget the sincerity of my father's declaration, as he was never one to wear his heart on his sleeve.

On leave with my parents.

After completing my training in Key West, I was assigned to the USS *Straub*, Destroyer Escort (DE) 181, and I picked up the ship in Brooklyn where commissioning ceremonies were held. My mother came to the commissioning, and we had a few days together during which time we saw a couple of live shows, including Louis Prima and his band, which both of us enjoyed. When she left for home I felt sad, but didn't realize that it would be the last time I would see her until the war was over.

I spent all of my time at sea, operating out of Recife, Brazil, tracking down German submarines, and was involved in sinking one after being out to sea fourteen months in the South Atlantic. I also spent ten months on a minesweeper, cleaning up mines along the coast from Virginia to Massachusetts.

During my time in active service, I received a letter from one of my first roommates at the University of Maine, John Shurtleff, telling me that he had joined the U.S. Air Force and was stationed temporarily in Atlantic City, New Jersey. Within a month I received a letter from John's mother advising me that John was dead. Mrs. Shurtleff provided no details as to the cause of his death, but I learned years later that John had been the victim of an infectious serum with which he and others had been injected during their training period.

Months later, I received another letter, from the mother of my other Orono roommate, Freddie Harrison, saying that he had been killed in action. He had joined the navy about the same time that I had, and had become a navy corpsman assigned to the U.S. Marine Corps, which brought him to the invasion of Iwo Jima in the Pacific where his life came to an end. Freddie and I had corresponded with each other during the war; in fact, in his last letter he had stated, "This is hell on earth . . . if I ever survive, it will be a miracle." Freddie's miracle never happened. I still have that letter.

Many years after the war, my wife and I had occasion to visit Honolulu, Hawaii. From the registry of the Punch Bowl Cemetery, I discovered that Freddie's remains were buried there with so many others who had lost their lives in that theater. His gravesite was directly next to the grave of the famous World War II correspondent, Ernie Pyle. I paid my respects to a great "roomie" and took pictures of the gravesite.

I was discharged from the U.S. Navy at the Fargo Building in Boston, and I couldn't wait to get home after being away for nearly three years. I was excited and nervous as I got off the bus in Madawaska and ran down the hill at 15th Avenue to the front door of my home. A sense of apprehension seized me as I opened the front door and saw my mother standing in the kitchen. She had aged so much! Her hair, which had always had a soft brown tinge, was now dull gray. Her face was still round and plump, and that Irish twinkle in her eye had not changed, but I had trouble recognizing her voice when I heard it for the first time in months. Still,

During World War II, I served in the U.S. Navy aboard the USS Straub, DE 181.

her voice was filled with happiness, and I wrapped my arms around her, saying nothing as I held her ever so close. Both of us were tearing up, so glad that we were together again at last.

As she spoke, her voice was weak, with a tone of sadness. She had been too long away from her only child, and she had worried and suffered in my absence. (She later admitted that she had said her rosary and prayed every day for my safety. I told her that I had prayed to God daily also, that he would keep my parents alive and well, and that they would be there when I got home.)

It wasn't long before my father came home from work. As soon as he came through the front door and saw me, he grabbed me into his arms and held me harder than I could ever remember. Nothing was said, but his eyes said it all. They welled up with tears, as did mine. Silently we stood embracing each other for several minutes until my father pushed away, looked into my eyes, and said, "Welcome home, son."

Chapter Twenty

Adjusting to Civilian Life

Many questions and decisions faced me during the summer of 1946. What did I want to do for the rest of my life? What studies appealed to me? How could I best use the GI Bill to finance my education? Did I wish to return to the University of Maine or apply to a more prestigious university? The answers to these questions caused me considerable anxiety as I struggled to decide who I was, and what I wanted to be.

I did not come up with immediate answers to these questions, and so eventually relaxed and chummed around with friends, who had just returned from the war, too. We enjoyed getting together to talk about our experiences over the past three or four years. The war had made us young men, and we became close. Age differences were no longer as important as they once were in high school. We often pursued the same women and we would kibitz over a beer and describe our various love conquests. It was a man's paradise that first summer at home, as many of the women in town had lost their loved ones or had been without the companionship of men for some time. They seemed anxious and eager to renew love relationships with any man who felt the same way, so most of us took advantage of the situation and bragged at our nightly meetings in the local pubs about how many times we had "scored."

Many of my postwar love affairs occurred in Edmundston, which required transportation. My father allowed me to use his car whenever I had planned a date. My travel area was restricted, however, by regulations of the Canadian Customs. To drive outside of the town limits of Edmundston, it was necessary to obtain a permit and advise customs officials of one's destination. I had arranged for a date with a young attractive married woman whose husband, at that time, had not been discharged from the Canadian Army. I had not intended to go outside city limits, but, once my date was in the car, it became obvious that she wanted to find a secluded country road outside of the city.

I gave no thought to getting a permit and drove my father's car in the direction of St. Basile, a small community a few miles south of Edmundston. As we drove along the main highway, I turned onto a narrow dirt road that went off at a right angle from the road we were traveling, and after going about a half-mile, came to a railroad track that ran parallel to the main highway. As I crossed over the track, the front and the back wheels of the car got hung up over the rails with both tires sinking into the gravel beds of the track. Earlier summer rains had softened the bed, and the car was stuck. We were stranded!

The track was an active one, and I knew that each evening about nine-thirty, a freight train would barrel into Edmundston from the south. I frantically dug into the gravel railroad bed until my hands and fingers were skinned and bleeding, to no avail. The car would not move, no matter how much I moved the gravel around to assist the wheels over the track.

My only hope was to walk back to the main road and seek help. I instructed my date to stay in the car and remain calm. If she saw a train approaching, she was to remove herself from the car and get back up the road a safe distance from the collision that would happen. As I walked back to the road I imagined the freight train striking and demolishing my father's car, and the ramifications of breaking the law by leaving the city without a permit. There would be publicity in the local papers. Oh, my God, I thought, I'm ruined! As I left to look for help, my date was crying, screaming, and cursing me all in one breath and was no help whatsoever.

A miracle happened that night. I had no sooner reached the road when a large Imperial Oil truck approached me as I stood waving frantically. The truck stopped. I explained to the driver my predicament and without hesitation, he said, "I'll get you out." He backed the truck down that narrow dirt road for about a half-mile, dragged out a chain, hooked it under my back bumper and pulled the car off the track. I never had much money on me in those days but I offered him everything I had in my wallet. He refused to take anything. I was so excited and relieved that I had avoided what could have been a disaster that I failed to even ask his name, but I thanked him over and over.

Needless to say, I couldn't get back to Edmundston quick enough. I discharged my date, who was more than glad to get rid of me. I didn't even get a kiss good night.

I had another incident with my father's car that fall. Once I had curbed any desire for dating married women, I began dating a lovely girl from Madawaska. The parents of my new love didn't care for me because of our religious differences. We enjoyed each other's company and dated without her parents' approval. Her parents should never have worried, as this friend of mine had a good head on her shoulders, and she was extremely bright and sensible. Our intimacy never went beyond kissing, although we did our share of that.

Our favorite parking place was located in an apple orchard off the main highway between Madawaska and Frenchville. The farmer who owned the land didn't appreciate us parking in his orchard, and he occasionally came over to the car and asked us to leave. To keep him from knowing that we were in his orchard, I would often turn off the car lights before reaching the orchard entrance and coast to a stop. I avoided braking to prevent the red taillights from coming on.

This plan worked well until one moonless night when my friend and I drove to the orchard, and I turned off the car lights just before the entrance. We coasted into the orchard and suddenly came to a loud and abrupt stop, short of our usual stopping area. We had run into a potato-digging machine, which the farmer had left in the middle of the road. The impact smashed in the front grill of my father's car. Needless to say, my father was not particularly happy about the incident.

The mishap with the potato digger prevented my friend and I from returning to the orchard, and we soon stopped seeing each other on a regular basis. I never knew whether it was this incident that cooled our relationship, but it certainly cooled my father's willingness to let me use his car whenever I wanted.

Chapter Twenty-One

G-8 and His Battle Aces

It seemed that the longer I was home after my discharge from the navy, the more I annoyed my father with my scatterbrained activities. I had already lost the use of his car for more than one reason, and now I was in trouble again.

I had a summer job with Fraser Paper Company and was assigned to work in the beater room, over which my father was superintendent. It was my responsibility to regulate the flow of raw stock that was manufactured in Fraser's pulp mill in Edmundston. The watered stock was pumped to the paper mill in Madawaska through large pipes attached to the International Bridge. The pulp was pumped into large vats that were below the floor of the beater room. Then, it was pumped again onto what was called an Oliver Press, which would suction most of the water out and leave a large sheet of semi-moist pulp on the barrel of the press.

I regulated the flow of stock with control switches that would prevent the lower vats from overflowing. I also adjusted the speed of the flowing pulp as it collected on the Oliver Press, as the pulp could jam the press if the flow was not properly regulated. I also regulated the amount of caustic soda that would be added to the wet pulp. The job was far from strenuous. I sat in a chair overlooking the press, and from there I manipulated the control valves to maintain a proper flow of the pulp for most of the eight hours of my shift. I sat alone in an empty room, and the job was boring. Time passed slowly, especially on the midnight to eight o'clock shift. I began to bring reading materials with me to ease the boredom of constant vigilance over the control levers as I watched stock cascade down over the Oliver Press.

One midnight shift, I became engrossed in reading a story from the popular pulp magazine, *G-8 and His Battle Aces*. As I read it, I lost all sense of time and responsibility. My father arrived for work about the time my shift was ending. Instead of his usual good morning hello, he let out an oath loud enough to be heard in the pulp mill in Edmundston, I'm sure. When I looked up, I couldn't believe what I was seeing. The storage vats had overflowed, and barrels of caustic soda and other chemicals were floating around the stock room. The stock had risen at least two feet above the floor level.

My father immediately closed the stock room door so the stock couldn't flow out to the beater room, handed me a shovel and hollered, "Move it, and get every g—d— bit of stock back into the vats." I moved it, and I shoveled and shoveled for the whole morning, until finally every bit of the overflowed stock was back in the vats. I had to do all the shoveling myself; my father, who seemed to watch me with great amusement, would not allow my shift replacement to lift a hand to help. I should have been fired on the spot. At home that evening, my father lectured me on the meaning of responsibility. For not firing me, I owed him one. Over the remaining years of his life, I owed him many more for his kindness, love, and understanding of my mistakes.

As the summer of 1946 was drawing to an end, I had to make up my mind what courses I would take when I returned to the University of Maine. My ultimate decision was influenced by a book I had read while at sea in the navy. It was entitled *Days of Our Years* and was written by Pierre Van Passen, a Dutchman. I borrowed it from the U.S. naval facility in Bahia, Brazil, and I never returned it. It probably provoked me more than any book I had read before, because it made me believe that young men in World War I gave their lives—not for love of country, necessarily, but for industrial and corporate profits.

Van Passen wrote that Germany had based its calculations on a swiftly moving war with a supply of war stocks that would have carried her through a year of war on two fronts. The Allies would have defeated Germany by the end of 1915. However, the Reich was receiving an uninterrupted supply of contraband goods from various sources. Secret meetings were being held to inhibit bombing attacks on key German targets, prolonging the war in the interest of profits for the corporations that were providing the required supplies. It was the greed of large corporations throughout the world that extended the war to four years rather than just one (when it could have been stopped), and as World War I continued unnecessarily, countless young men died—including my mother's brother, my would-be uncle.

When I first finished reading *Days of Our Years* I was furious, and I decided that should I survive the war, I would become an activist against warmongers and men of means who would sacrifice human lives for their own personal financial gain. I believed at the time that the only way to curb this corruption was to play some role in the political process, or to become a participant in the administration of our country's government. How naive I was to believe that government was without corruption.

I read the book several times, focusing on other passages that blamed the DuPonts of America for their part in extending World War I. I thought of my father, who had suffered hardships in the battles of Ypres, Vimy Ridge, and the Somme, France. He believed he was fighting overseas for God and Country. He fought in France and Germany from 1915 until the Armistice was signed in 1918. He could have been living the best years of his life with friends and family during those years instead. I was also enraged when I thought of my mother's youngest brother, my Uncle Barney, whom I had never known, being killed at the Battle of the Somme not too many days before the Armistice was signed with Germany. Had the war ended sooner, as it could have, he would have lived and returned to his family in New Brunswick. I thought back to my freshman year in college, and my two roommates, Johnnie Shurtleff and Freddie Harrison, both now dead because of their military service in World War II. It angered me to think that they too had lost the best years of their lives. *Days of Our Years* made me think of my own life. While at sea week after week, always with some risk, I'd wonder whether men of financial wealth connected with corporate businesses were running this war as well. Were the DuPonts still getting richer at the expense of sacrificing young American lives?

Van Passen's story affected my decision as to what studies I would pursue at college. My best option in the fall of 1946 at the university was a course in political science and public administration, under the direction of Dr. Edward F. Dow. While the degree program did not completely satisfy my desire to become involved in national and international issues, it did provide an opportunity for participation in local government. I returned to the University of Maine, and three years later, received my bachelor of arts degree in public administration.

More important than earning my degree in those three years following the war, however, was my love affair with Shirley Smith, who had enrolled as a freshman at the University of Maine in the fall of 1947.

Shirley and I dated throughout my last two years of college, until, upon my graduation, I moved to Syracuse, New York, to enter Syracuse University's Maxwell School of Citizenship's graduate program of political science. This program was in keeping with my earlier and constant desire to become involved with federal issues.

At Syracuse, I was assigned a proctor's position in a college rooming home for men, but I was relocated three times between September and the Christmas holidays. These moves were causing me problems in meeting the demands of my coursework.

I kept in constant touch with Shirley by phone, sometimes to her parents' consternation as our phone conversations often took place in the wee hours of the morning. After my third relocation, I decided to leave Syracuse. I called Shirley and asked her to marry me. She said "yes."

Before I left for Syracuse in the fall of 1949, I had been offered a position as town manager of Madawaska after my college graduation from the University of Maine, but I had turned down the job to pursue my graduate studies. After Shirley accepted my proposal, I called the Madawaska town office to see if the job was still available. It was. I came back to Maine, leaving my chances to obtain an advanced degree in political science behind. I interviewed again for the town manager's position, and was appointed before my wedding date.

Shirley and I were married on January 22, 1950, in her family home in Hampden Highlands, Maine, and then we were off to Madawaska. I was back in the Land of the Porcupine with my new bride and a new job.

Chapter Twenty-Two

Married Life

Fate has played an important role throughout my life. It was fate that I had decided to terminate my graduate studies and return home. It was fate that the town manager's job in Madawaska was available to me at a time when I needed a job very badly. Levite Rossignol, a well-known insurance agent in town, was chairman of the board of selectmen. He knew my parents, and indirectly knew me. He was considered an astute politician, was blunt in stating his opinions, and was not always well liked by many taxpayers. Somewhat apprehensively I asked to meet with him, in hopes that he would recommend me as the town's new manager.

I suspect he checked my reputation in the community, and when he didn't find too many negative disclosures in my past, he offered me the appointment. I owe a debt of gratitude to him for having enough confidence in me to give me my first real job.

I must admit that when I assumed my duties at the town office, I was still wet behind the ears, very nervous, and somewhat doubtful that I could face up to the problems of my hometown or any town. My courses in public management related primarily to theories of organizational structures, management styles, and a multitude of other theoretical situations that did not seem to apply to the real world. I was on the job less than two weeks when I realized that I was "up to my ass in alligators." My position as town manager also entailed a number of other roles. I was the town treasurer and tax collector, the road commissioner and the manager of the town-owned water company. I also found out very quickly that I was the town's welfare director, a job about which I knew absolutely nothing. The concerns of the poor and needy and how to respond to claims for assistance—or the laws pertaining to the same—were never discussed or taught in my university studies. I was never taught the mentality of those in need and how to determine if demands for assistance were legitimate or not.

I married Shirley Ann (Smith) in 1950.

I never enjoyed my role as welfare director. I had a soft heart when it came to a sad story of child neglect or abuse by a drunken spouse, even when I knew that I was being conned. I believe that over the years, I have heard every possible story that could be told by folks wanting town support. Every time I got taken advantage of and relented to someone's request, I paid the price, as invariably I would be approached by someone else who would expect the same results for the same story. It always amazed me that, even though none of the welfare recipients had telephones and often lived many miles apart without any means of transportation, they would know immediately what went on at the town office; who had received a handout and for what amount. I often imagined that they must have somehow sent secret messages to each other using smoke signals or devised some other means of communication known only to them.

It took me many months in my position as town manager to recognize the various methods that welfare recipients used to surmount my denials to their requests. I must admit, however, there were times when I got outwitted by their demands. If nothing else, they were professionals in convincing me of their needs. Be that as it may, I did overcome my vulnerability in time.

In the latter part of February 1950, I had been married a month and was in a state of bliss with my new bride. This must have lessened my sensitivity to the number of problems I faced on a daily basis at work.

There is one event I will never forget. One cold day in February, I received a telephone call advising me that two small children had been abandoned in a house on one of the rural roads within the town limits. I wasn't sure what to do, so I called the chief of police into my office and suggested we both drive to the home to verify the call.

Fedime (pronounced *Fi'Jim*) Morin was Madawaska's police chief during my tenure as town manager—the same chief who had considered arresting me as a youngster when I "borrowed" the handcar from the B & A. He was an exceptional law enforcement officer, and in my many years as a manager in other communities, I have never found his equal. Fedime had a limited formal education, but possessed great common sense.

Two small toddlers were looking out the window of the house as we drove into the driveway. They wore nothing but diapers, but although the home was a cool 45 degrees, they seemed no worse for their neglect. From what the chief and I could discern, they had not been fed for some time and had probably been alone for at least thirty-six hours. The chief retrieved a blanket from his cruiser, wrapped the children in it and took them to the next-door neighbor's house requesting that they care for the children until we could locate the parents. They willingly did so.

We returned to the town office, where the chief immediately made several telephone calls and returned to my office. He said he had a pretty good idea where he could find the parents, and asked that I go along to assist him. We drove toward Fort Kent, and when we got to a point where the B & A tracks crossed Route 1 in Upper Frenchville, the Chief pulled into a side road and drove until we came to a small camp hidden back in the woods. What I witnessed was my first behind-the-scenes view of what goes on in a community such as this. It would not be the last such encounter, either, as all communities have their hidden secrets.

As Fedime and I entered the cabin's unlocked front door, four naked persons scrambled from the one bed in the cabin, grabbing whatever they could find to cover themselves.

We had abruptly terminated a wife-swapping orgy that was still in progress. After sufficiently reprimanding the couples, the chief quickly escorted them back to their homes. In no uncertain terms, he had put the fear of God, and of himself, into each one of them.

Madawaska is a mill town, and Thursday was payday. It wasn't long after the workers received their checks that the local bars were fully engaged, and every Thursday night (as well as Friday and Saturday nights) was a tough night for the local police. Although Fedime was not required to work night shifts, one could be assured that he would be around when the drinking in town was more intense. He wasn't there to arrest drinkers, however. He knew everyone in town and was there to protect them from injury and possible death. If he thought a patron leaving a tavern was too inebriated to drive, Fedime would ask for his keys and drive him home, suggesting that the keys could be picked up at the police station the next morning. Fedime stood well over six feet tall and spoke with authority, but gently, so very few ever disagreed with his suggestion.

My wife and I lived on the second floor of Roy's Apartment House on Eleventh Avenue. From our kitchen window we could look directly into the apartment across the way in the neighboring building on Main Street. It was occupied by a young couple about our age, and they were also probably recently married, because they faithfully made love each evening about nine o'clock. Whether they couldn't afford blinds or shades for their windows or just didn't care, we never knew, but none were drawn. It also was their habit to go to bed with the lights on. Very soon, most of our friends were told about the nightly entertainment program that could be seen from our kitchen window. Some friends would gather in our kitchen with the lights out and kibitz on the performance from one night to the next.

A peeping Tom soon discovered the same entertainment and began to show up nightly with a ladder that he placed against the neighboring building. He would climb to a rung so his eyes were just above the windowsill. He had a prime position for viewing. Although I guess, in retrospect, my wife and I and our friends weren't much better than the peeping Tom, I still reported "Tom" to the police chief, who advised me that he would handle the situation. One evening as my wife and I were observing the "peeper," but at the same time keeping an eye on the bedroom action, we noticed a mill worker walking down the street with a lunch pail under his arm. Suddenly, the lunch bucket was dropped, and the worker came racing down the alley between the two buildings and pulled the intruder from his position on the ladder. The worker escorted "Tom" back to the street, and as he did so, we recognized the worker to be the police chief. Fedime had taken care of the matter.

Shortly after our marriage, I purchased a black-and-tan coonhound. On most weekends when it was legal to hunt rabbits, my father and I would take the hound, which we had named "Sleepy," and head into the woods with friends who also had hunting dogs. We would run the dogs from morning until night. There were days when we couldn't get the dogs off the scent of a rabbit and would have to leave them overnight. We would go back the next day to retrieve them. I would always leave my hunting jacket as a sign that I would be back. Whether or not the dog understood this, I was never sure, but he was always curled up on my hunting jacket when we returned to get him, and was ready to jump into my car and go home.

I was very attached to Sleepy. Occasionally, he would team up with another beagle that was owned by Dana McKay, a neighbor, and they would strike off by themselves to a nearby wooded area and chase rabbits until they tired. Often when Sleepy would return from one of these jaunts, he would crawl behind the kitchen stove and sleep for two or three days. On one occasion, Sleepy didn't return at the time we expected him. After a couple of days had passed, I knew that something must have happened to him, and I went looking in the general area that he usually hunted. My concerns were well-founded. It wasn't long before I spotted him lying at the base of a large pine tree, on some pine needles that were soaked in blood. He had been shot! His beagle friend, who had also been fatally shot, was lying beside Sleepy.

My wife and I were grief-stricken, and we cried for a good part of the remainder of the day. The next morning, I reported my findings to Fedime, who was also a dog lover. Fedime had raised a Saint Bernard and taught him to raise the flag at the town office each morning, to fetch the mail at the post office, and other useful tricks. He was a remarkable dog trainer and never spoke harshly to any dog. Fedime immediately understood my grief. After hearing from me where I had found the dogs, he said, very matter-of-factly, "I think I know who might have done this."

We drove to a farmhouse on the Frenchville Road. The farmer was in a field planting potatoes. Fedime stepped out of the police cruiser and said to the man, "What was the color of those two dogs you shot the other day?" I didn't expect the man to answer, but he did. He said that one dog was black and tan, and the other was black, tan and white. Fedime then cited him.

We were paid the price of replacing Sleepy with another black-and-tan coonhound. We named our new dog Smokey, but he never measured up to Sleepy. Eventually, we had to give Smokey away, as he didn't have the same temperament as his predecessor and disliked being around children.

I, and I'm sure many others, have so many fond memories of Fedime Morin, who remained Madawaska's police chief until his death, of natural causes. He knew the community and the people of that locality better than most, and through that gift, kept order without incident.

My first year as a municipal manager broadened my perspective of my position in the community. I soon saw how politics could play a part in jeopardizing my career.

In most communities, there are influential citizens, or power brokers, who impact the activities of local government. Some are easily identified, but there are others who hide behind the actions of others. Many suggested to me, at the time that I applied for the position of town manager of Madawaska, that my authority as manager would be ignored by the first selectman, Levite Rossignol. It was indicated to me early in my new position that I should do as the first selectman suggested, or I wouldn't remain as the town manager for very long. However, at the university, I had been taught very strongly by Dr. Edward Dow that I should never compromise my beliefs or commitment if a problem was well analyzed. I followed that advice to arrive at decisions that I thought were best for the community.

Having heard of Mr. Rossignol's influence in the community, I fully expected the first selectman to become a problem. My fears were unfounded, however, as Mr. Rossignol was extremely supportive and never attempted to influence any of my decisions. Quite to the contrary; in fact, he would often advise me what reactions to expect from the taxpayers about programs I proposed.

In many instances, his input on major issues provided me with food for thought, allowing me to think things through again, and be better prepared to answer the arguments that generally arose with every issue that involved money. I learned very quickly from him that for every action, there is a reaction. He provided me with a keen insight into local politics and taught me how to cope with the emotional fears of taxpayers. A mentor in political science is a much better teacher than a textbook. I am greatly indebted to a man whom I thought I would fear, but instead came to respect and admire.

Chapter Twenty-Three

Our First Child, Judith Denise

Shortly after my first year as town manager of Madawaska had been completed, my wife gave birth to our first child, Judith Denise. A doctor friend of mine (who was also my golfing companion) had treated Shirley throughout her pregnancy. As an osteopathic doctor, he wasn't always accepted for practice in medical facilities, but he had assured me that he had hospital privileges and could deliver our baby when the time arrived.

Shirley began labor pains on the evening of January 10. At midnight I became somewhat nervous that the baby would arrive before I got my wife to the hospital, which was twenty-five miles away in Van Buren. We called our doctor so that he could notify the hospital we were on our way. When we arrived at the Hotel Dieu hospital, we were met by a nun at the front door who said no arrangements had been made for Shirley. The sister said our doctor would not be allowed to perform the delivery at her hospital. Somewhat panicked, I said that I didn't dare drive back to Madawaska at that late hour with Shirley in labor.

The nun said she would contact a local doctor. Being assured that Shirley would be in good hands, I left my wife and returned home to grab a few minutes of sleep, returning later that day. A good friend of ours, Ellen Demers, a nurse from Madawaska, went to the hospital to be with Shirley during the last stages of labor, and was a source of much comfort to her. At that time, husbands were not allowed into the delivery room. Judith was born at 8:30 P.M. on January 11, 1951.

When I first saw Judy, she was stretched out on a small table, with her backside up and her head bent to one side. She had a cute, round, perky face that touched my heart at first sight. She was the cutest little girl that I had ever seen. My wife, the most beautiful woman in my life, had come through the birth without a problem. She didn't even seem disturbed that the doctor who had attended to her throughout the nine months of pregnancy didn't show up for the delivery. Her attending doctor was a compassionate and skilled obstetrician from Van Buren.

Returning home that night, I went to my parents' home in Madawaska and was met by a group of friends who were there to give me a congratulating welcome. They tape-recorded the party so that Shirley might hear their words of happiness for us later.

The next day, home after visiting Shirley and the baby again, I was getting a bite to eat when there was a knock at the door. Months before my marriage, when I was attending Syracuse University, a U.S. government check was stolen from my mail. I had reported it to authorities, but I had not heard anything about it since. The man at my door was a T-man from the Federal Treasury Department. He had been assigned the recovery of my missing check. He came in, identified himself, and at my invitation sat at my kitchen table. Then he requested that I write my signature fifty times on a piece of paper that he handed me. I did and he left.

On the next night after my daily visit with Shirley (at that time new mothers were kept in the hospital about five days), I stopped at the bar of the Van Buren Hotel. I recognized the T-man at a nearby table, and he motioned for me to sit down with him. After a few minutes, I noticed that he had more drinks than he should have, and he began talking about his life as a T-man. He pulled a revolver out of a holster I hadn't seen before, and he placed it on the table. I made up a reason that I had to get back to the hospital and quickly left, returning home to Madawaska.

Eventually, I was reimbursed for my errant check, so the T-man must have sobered up and recommended that my stolen check be reissued. The week of my daughter's birth was more hectic and eventful than I had planned. I was still peeved that my golfing friend and Shirley's doctor had never shown up or made arrangements for Shirley's admittance at the Hotel Dieu in Van Buren. Shirley was more forgiving than I was about the doctor who had promised to deliver our first child. I had questioned him more than once about whether he as an osteopathic doctor would be allowed to assist my wife with her delivery in the Van Buren hospital, and he continued to say that he could. He assured me that there would be no problem. Even more strange was the fact that I never got an explanation as to why he was absent on a date that was very important to my wife and me. I had no choice but to accept what had happened, but never cared to play golf with him again.

Chapter Twenty-Four

Roger Berube, First Selectman

In 1952, during my second year as Madawaska's town manager, the town meeting and annual election of selectmen resulted in a surprise win for one of my closest friends, Roger Berube. Roger became the first selectman. We had grown up together, having lived not more than a quarter of a mile apart, and had joined the navy about the same time. Now we shared the responsibility of conducting the affairs of a town with a population of more than 5,000—small in some respects, but large when compared to the majority of other communities in Maine.

Both in our mid-twenties, our youthfulness was recognized in an article in the *Maine Sunday Telegram*. The article dealt with our teamwork and proposed improvement programs, and it tagged us both as aspiring and inspiring community leaders. Roger and I had initiated a new sewer system for the town; named all of the town streets, none of which had been officially named before; completed the town's first tax revaluation; constructed a town skating rink; and provided the incentive for the local Rotary Club to build a public swimming pool. We also introduced the town's first capital improvement budget.

Roger was bright. He came from limited means and had a devil-may-care attitude, but he had developed his own successful insurance business. In some ways, he was a hellion with suave ethnic good looks, but he always had a kind heart and was never without a smile. He was willing to take risks with his own business and felt that managing local government held certain risks as well. He was willing to support many of the ideas that I wanted to try.

When I suggested a revaluation—honestly believing in my own mind that the Fraser mill was underassessed and that a shift in property values would benefit the small homeowner—Roger, as well as the other two selectmen, supported me. When the final figures were completed by the Cole, Layer and Trumble Company, I learned very quickly that I was wrong. In fact, the study showed that the Fraser mill had been overassessed. There was a taxpayer's group in the town that was ready to "tar and feather" me. I was threatened by personal remarks and suggestions by groups, which you find in every community, that I should be removed from office. For an instant, I thought I had tossed my own position out the window. However, throughout my life, I have seen small miracles, and once again, one happened.

The Fraser Company, being a corporate good neighbor, saw the value of the revaluation of town properties, which hadn't been reviewed for years. Although it was to benefit through a sizeable reduction in its local taxes, the company told the town that its tax liabilities should not be decreased, and it would pay the same amount as in previous years. Because of that, the revaluation study was accepted by the townspeople; the shift of taxes from the mill to the local homeowner was avoided, and most important from my point of view, I remained on as town manager. The advantage, however, was that all properties, other than the mill, were adjusted to their true value, and the town's total valuation had increased, thus reducing the local tax rate, which residents paid more attention to than their property values.

At the time of my appointment as town manager, I was also appointed superintendent of the Madawaska Water Department. The salary at the time for both positions was $60 weekly, or $3,120 a year. Money didn't seem all that important then and I was happy with the pay, because I was happy with the position and what I was doing. Managing a town was more relaxing in the earlier years of the town management movement in Maine than it is now, and times of stress were evened out with just as many fun times. At least, I can look back now and smile—even laugh out loud—at some of our experiences.

When Roger and I devised a capital improvement program for the town, we included the purchase of a grader and the town's first backhoe. We were convinced that we could do the town's roadwork cheaper with our own manpower and equipment than hiring outside contractors. The price of the grader was $12,000, but the salesman advised me that the town would be invoiced for $13,000. I couldn't understand the logic behind his company's pricing policy, not realizing that the additional thousand dollars would be a personal rebate to me when the town paid the invoice. I was plenty "green" at the time, but when the salesman explained why the price was going to be invoiced higher than the agreed-upon purchasing price, I was infuriated and reported it to the board of selectmen. They agreed with me that a different vendor should provide the town with the machines. The word must have gone out to other suppliers because I was never approached again with even the slightest hint of a bribe, and I remained in the town management field for twenty-five years.

The purchase of the town's first backhoe is another story. Roger and I took a bus to Augusta, where the backhoe was purchased, to drive it back to Madawaska, thus saving the town transportation and delivery costs. After the money had changed hands, drinks were offered around. Since I knew that I would do most of the driving, I elected not to join in this occasion of goodwill and cheer. Roger decided otherwise, and after a couple more rounds of well wishing and congratulations, we headed for home.

I made the trip back in one day, but it took Roger two. When we arrived in Bangor, he decided to stay over. When I asked how he was going to get home, he assured me that it would be no problem. I left him at the Bangor House hotel and drove off for Madawaska. Roger's drinks must have been poured stiffer than he realized, because he told me later that he didn't recall much after he left Augusta, and couldn't figure out what he was doing at the Bangor House when he awakened the next morning. He never told me how he got home, and I didn't ask.

Roger and I both took our responsibilities to the town of Madawaska very seriously, but the chemistry we had between us when resolving problems on occasion led us off the straight and narrow path. Once in a while we would say to each other, "Let's loosen up and live a little!"

In one of those carefree moods, we were driving to Augusta to attend the annual meeting of the Maine Municipal Association. As we approached Bangor, Roger admitted, raising his hand to the top of his head, that he was "up to here with municipal problems." Then he said, "To hell with Augusta—let's you and I spend a couple of days in Montreal!"

My quick reply was, "You're the boss," and in Bangor, we switched directions and headed west instead of continuing south. We had our two days in Montreal, visiting several nightspots and watering holes. Then we headed back to Maine through the flat farmlands near Magog, Quebec. Roger always could consume more of the demon rum than I could, but he also tired more

While serving as town manager of Madawaska, I provided a weekly town report on WJEM, a New Brunswick radion station.

quickly. So again, I assumed the driving detail, but I grew tired as well. I picked a large open field to drive the car into, parked and grabbed a few winks of sleep in the front seat. Roger was asleep in the backseat, as he had been since we left Montreal.

It seemed that I had only been asleep but a few minutes, when I was aroused by Roger, shaking my shoulder and frantically shouting, "Ron, please wake up . . . Oh, my God . . . we're dead!" He kept repeating these words, until I realized what he was saying and sat up. "What's wrong?" I asked.

He replied, "I believe we're dead!" After I assured him that we were not dead but very much alive, he explained that when he awoke in the middle of the field, he looked out of the car and all he could see was a lot of sky, no houses, no trees—just flat land and lots of sky. He found me slumped over in the front seat and immediately assumed that we had been in an accident, and both of us had died and were in heaven. We laughed about this incident many times in later life.

Roger died of cancer at the young age of fifty-one in January of 1975, but I have a feeling that he occasionally looks down on that stretch of farmland near Magog and still has a good laugh.

My daily work as a town manager never failed to bring unexpected surprises. As I entered my office each day, I could never predict what might happen before the day ended.

On one particular afternoon, the police chief advised me of a man's attempted suicide that morning. The man's wife now wanted her husband committed to the mental hospital in Bangor. After checking the Maine statutes to determine my responsibilities in such a matter, I learned that the law allowed the board of selectmen to decide whether a person should be committed after an investigation and a public hearing was conducted. The board asked me to conduct the investigation prior to the hearing. The investigation was to consist of a standard set of questions put to people familiar with the subject's behavioral patterns.

I asked the man's wife to come to my office to shed some light as to why her husband would attempt to commit suicide. Her answers were quite shocking. She said she had found him in the barn, standing on a barrel, attempting to have intercourse with the family horse. Upon being discovered, he had cut his wrists and drank a glass of lime—calcium oxide, not the fruit—diluted with water. I couldn't believe what I was hearing, but even more surprising were her answers to the required questions about her husband's sexual habits. When asked if her husband had sexual relations with her, she said, "Oh yes, every night and sometimes twice or more per night!"

After the interview, I thought to myself, "And he still had enough energy to take care of the family horse as well—unbelievable!"

Chapter Twenty-Five

Good Times Remembered

I have no bad memories of that time in my life, only good ones—like the time I shot my first deer. Armand Bosse and I hunted in the area around Estcourt, Quebec, the same town where I had been conceived. One year, there was a hoof-and-mouth disease epidemic, and there was a restriction against bringing any hoofed animal across the border. To reach Estcourt, it was necessary to leave Maine, drive a short distance through the provinces of New Brunswick and Quebec, and then back into Maine, where the town of Estcourt was situated in Quebec near the border, at the tip of a part of Maine that jutted north.

For the first time, I was fortunate enough to bring one down. Then we said, "What do we do with it?" The carcass of the deer had to remain on American soil, so we hid it and holed up in Blue River, Quebec, until we could figure out a way to get it back home. No way was I going to leave my first deer behind!

The St. Francis River was the only way we could transport the deer back to Maine without entering Canada, so we traveled back to Maine, where I got my car and headed for St. Francis, Maine. Meanwhile, Armand got a friend and a canoe, went back to where my deer was hidden, loaded it into the canoe, paddled down the St. Francis River to St. Francis, where we unloaded the deer onto the fender of my car. When we got back to Madawaska, I was so proud of that deer, I drove around for so long with the carcass on the hood of my car that I think the meat started to spoil.

I have another memory of a hunting incident. A new chemist had been employed at the mill, and he had a fondness for hunting. When the hunting season came, he wanted to hunt with us, but couldn't afford the cost of a rifle. We told him he could borrow a rifle from Leon Cyr, who we knew owned more than one. Leon was reluctant to lend a rifle, saying, halfkidding, "I would rather loan my wife than my rifle." We assured him that the person who would use his rifle was responsible, and the rifle would be carefully handled and returned in the same condition in which it was received.

Our new acquaintance had beginner's luck in the woods of Maine, and his first morning out, as he was walking down a tote road, a large buck stepped out in front of him. He fired and the buck went down, but, as he cautiously approached the wounded deer, it attempted to get up. In his excitement, our friend—who should have considered shooting the deer again—instead took the rifle and began striking the deer on the head with the barrel of the gun. The deer expired, but the barrel of the rifle had been badly bent! It was difficult to explain to Leon what had happened, but the friend resolved the problem by buying him a new rifle.

There were also some practical jokes. I'd been part of many in my single days, and continued the tradition in my new job. One of my women friends from my single days, for instance, was not considered a good cook. One evening, when she had a group of friends over, myself included, she served a chocolate cake for dessert. Some ingredient must have been overlooked, as it was tasteless. The men present didn't want to hurt or embarrass the hostess, so someone wrapped the cake in a napkin and stuffed it into a pocket of his coat. For weeks afterwards the same piece of cake was mailed from one man to another, with a note expressing that it was understood the recipient had enjoyed the cake so much, a second piece was in the offing.

Then there was the time that another friend had just begun his law practice in town. He was a bachelor and was known to party considerably. One morning, we saw that his office door was unopened, so we knew that he must have been feeling quite rough. By then it was already mid-morning, and we visualized him in the office with the blinds drawn and his head in his hands. Across from his office was the local undertaker, so we borrowed a mourning wreath and hung it on the lawyer's office door. The wreath had a sign on it saying REST IN PEACE.

The undertaker, Mr. Daigle, was quite a prankster as well. A prominent businessman had expired, and his wife had purchased a very expensive suit in which her husband would be buried. Mr. Daigle had employed a young man during the summer to assist him in preparing the deceased bodies for burial. The young man he had just hired was known as a "French Jumper"—the expression used to describe a person with a nervous condition that causes him to react to a quick motion made by another person. If one quickly jumps toward a "jumper," the jumper will react by repeating the action, or by jumping toward the other person. I have never been given a reason for this condition, but I have personally seen individuals in Madawaska who had this affliction.

Mr. Daigle was explaining to his assistant that he would shove the deceased man's arm through the sleeve of the suit, carefully cautioning the assistant to be careful and not tear the sleeve, as the suit was very expensive. He told the assistant to grab the hand of the deceased when it began to exit from the sleeve. As he was talking to his helper, he knelt and secretly dipped his hand into a bucket of cold water. Then he put his own hand into the sleeve. When the young man reached for the hand inside the sleeve of the suit he began tugging on the cold hand and then felt it squeeze his hand. Needless to say, there was an immediate reaction, and the "jumper" not only jumped, he ran out of the room going through the screen door without even opening it.

Chapter Twenty-Six

Father Cyr and Father Menard

As I met the varied, daily challenges of my job, my daughter, Judy, was growing fast and at peace with her mother and me.

Although we were not Catholic, a local priest, Father Cyr, called on us regularly and showed an interest in our young one. I enjoyed Father Cyr's visits. We would discuss religion, local government and a variety of topics over a cup of tea and goodies that Shirley would prepare. Father Cyr and I became very close friends, and on one occasion, during the Lenten season, he asked me to be the guest speaker at the Knights of Columbus Easter breakfast.

I was never certain if he knew I had joined the Masonic Lodge in Fort Kent, but at the time I thought it highly unusual for a Mason to be the honored guest at a Knights of Columbus gathering, especially in the St. John Valley at a time long before the faiths had liberalized their feelings toward each other. However, I had been asked by a friend to attend, and as a friend I accepted.

On the day of the breakfast, a slight problem arose. A gentleman, who had had something to drink besides coffee for breakfast it seemed, stood and questioned why a Protestant was invited to the Knights of Columbus Easter Breakfast. Father Cyr rose very calmly, quietly apologized to me, approached the man, took him by the arm and led him out. I understood why a Protestant attending a Catholic organization function might be questioned, so it didn't bother me, but I appreciated what Father Cyr did, and there were no further problems. I gave my speech, and many of the group approached me afterward with positive comments.

My religious difference to the majority of the local residents was never questioned at any other time that I can recall in my twenty-eight years of residency in Madawaska.

Father Menard was the senior priest at the Thomas Aquinas Rectory. He was older than Father Cyr by many years, and his experiences were many. He often told me about them whenever we met. Although he never called at my home, as did Father Cyr, we met regularly at the post office, where we seemed to arrive each day about the same time. Father Menard had "class" and drove a large black Cadillac. The interior of his large sedan was divided by a screen that separated the front seat from the backseat, and the backseat housed a small black bulldog who went everywhere with Father Menard.

One morning, he pulled up in front of the post office and joined in my conversation with two French-speaking gentlemen from town. As we were talking, the bulldog was yelping and barking from the backseat of the car. Father Menard stopped talking suddenly, looked at his dog and loudly yelled at him, "Shut up, you Frenchman!" I know that my face flushed red, as I was quite taken aback and embarrassed upon hearing his unusual command to his dog.

It surprised me no end that when I decided to leave Madawaska, I received a personal letter from Father Menard. Although we had had many short conversations, I never sensed the same feeling of friendship that had grown between me and Father Cyr. Father Menard never called me by my first name, and yet he wrote the following when it was announced that I had taken a new position in Brewer, Maine:

My Dear Ronnie,

I frankly must state that I was stunned when I read in the Bangor Daily News *that you were leaving Madawaska. We will miss you. I liked the spirit and manner in which you take care of town affairs. I thank you for all you have done on our behalf. Your cooperation has been perfect. I wish you the best of success in your new assignment; and may God shower down his blessings upon you and your family.*

That letter meant a lot to me and I have kept it ever since.

Chapter Twenty-Seven

The Land of the Porcupine

The letter from Father Menard came after my fourth year as Madawaska's town manager. In 1953, as my family was expanding and I felt the need for a larger paycheck, I decided to apply for a manager's position in another town.

In the early part of that year, my wife had given birth to our first son, Gordon. We decided this baby would be born at a new hospital in Fort Kent, some twenty miles up the St. John River in the opposite direction from Van Buren, where our daughter had been born. On a cold winter evening in January, Roger Berube and I had attended a selectmen's meeting, after which the two of us stood on Main Street for well over an hour, discussing town affairs. Unbeknownst to us, my wife had been trying to locate me by phone. She had started feeling labor pains, and was extremely anxious, which I recognized immediately as I entered the front door of my home.

My wife had called my mother, who had already reached our house and was preparing to watch over our daughter, Judy. Within minutes of my arrival at home, I had Shirley into our car and on her way to Fort Kent. Our son, Gordon, was born within an hour after we reached the hospital, a little too close of a call for comfort. I was a proud father, having sired a boy, but I was somewhat alarmed by our newborn son's yellowish color. The nuns at the hospital assured me there was nothing to worry about, but I was still concerned. I was even more concerned to find that when my wife was well enough to leave the hospital, our son could not leave with us but would be detained until his color returned to normal.

My wife and I didn't learn the reason for the skin discoloration until nearly two years later when my wife became pregnant for the third time. It was determined then that my wife and I had an Rh factor, which meant that our blood types were not compatible. At the time, we had no idea that health problems could result for the baby. We were questioned quite extensively about the two earlier pregnancies. When we described the color of our son's skin at birth, our doctor said we were fortunate our son had lived, and that someone must have provided tender loving care during this critical period.

The tender loving care had been provided by the nuns at the Fort Kent Hospital. During our son's detainment at the hospital, they had injected him with a form of gamma globulin, somewhat similar to a blood transfusion. We didn't understand then the seriousness of his condition. We have thanked the nuns many times over for the life of our son.

Having a second child meant that we needed a car larger than our small coupe. We traded for a Chrysler Royal at the exorbitant price of $2,200. At the time, I didn't know how we were ever going to make ends meet. Somehow we did, but it became difficult, and I realized that I needed to find a higher-paying position. I knew it would only be a matter of time before we would be having another child, as my wife and I had pretty much decided that we wanted four children.

I was lucky enough to be selected for the city manager job in Brewer, about 200 miles south. I had mixed feelings and was reluctant to leave Madawaska, where I had grown up and had worked for the past four years. I was about to leave the Land of the Porcupine.

The town of Madawaska had been good to me. It had accepted me directly out of the University of Maine without any experience except for a summer internship under the very capable direction of Camden's town manager, Percy Keller, in 1948. The Madawaska Board of Selectmen worked closely with me during my development and often overlooked my weaknesses, especially concerning the management of welfare programs. The selectmen and I worked well as a team, and we were socially compatible. Often we would adjourn to the National Hotel in Madawaska after a meeting for a drink together. No one ever criticized the town manager for having a drink in public; in fact, in such a friendly community, I believe I would have been criticized more if I had refused to do so.

I hated to leave my hometown, and with my parents still living there, it was even harder. Many of my school friends were still my friends, everyone knew everyone, and I knew more than most. No one was especially wealthy, but we had everything we needed. We worked hard but we also played hard. No one called ahead to see if you were home or doing anything before they decided to visit; they would just come over and walk in without knocking and no one objected. Maybe there was more drinking and partying than there should have been in this free-spirited community, but it never became uncontrollable.

Shirley and I also thought of our children. Judy, while playing with her French-speaking little friends, was beginning to speak French. As for Shirley herself, she had easily adapted to the friendliness of the town, although it was much different than her younger days growing up near Cleveland, Ohio. She learned to love the town as much as I did. We had so many wonderful friends in Madawaska, and also in Edmundston across the river. . . . So many wonderful memories.

But, as difficult as it was, we decided to leave Madawaska. The future of our family became more important than the good times and the camaraderie of a small town we loved dearly.

And so, we left the Land of the Porcupine and took up residence in Brewer, Maine.

Epilogue

My wife and I had two more children while living in Brewer, Maine. Nancy was born in 1955, and Douglas was born in 1956, both at Eastern Maine General Hospital in Bangor.

All have done well with their own lives. Judy, our first child, lives in Simsbury, Connecticut, and has a degree in art history from the University of Hartford. As I publish this story of the Land of the Porcupine, she is back in college to obtain a law degree at the University of Connecticut Law School.

Gordon, our oldest son, lives in West Chester, Pennsylvania, and has his own law firm, Stewart and Associates, in Wilmington, Delaware. He got his degrees from Dartmouth College, Washington and Lee Law School and New York University Law School.

Nancy lives in Bath, Maine, and has a bachelor's degree in fine arts from Temple University in Philadelphia and a master's degree in literacy from the University of Southern Maine. She is a teacher at the Dike-Newell School in Bath.

Douglas is in southwestern New Hampshire and works as chief information officer for a casualty property company. He obtained an associate's degree in business at the University of Southern Maine.

Our four children in Brewer, 1956. (l-r) Douglas, Nancy, Gordon and Judith.

I am very proud of our four children.

The places where I've lived and worked differ widely, and the people I've met and worked with have varied personalities. The people of the St. John Valley, as I remember from when I lived there, have strong family bonds, a reverence for the Church, and a good feeling about life. They make time to smell the roses. I feel certain that those who live there today are much the same as when my wife, our children and I lived there. I am grateful for having spent nearly a third of my life in the Land of the Porcupine.

About the Author

Ron Stewart was born in the Province of New Brunswick, Canada. He moved to the United States with his parents when he was one year old.

He began school in Edmundston, New Brunswick, and graduated from Edmundston High School at age seventeen in 1942. That same year he entered the University of Maine in Orono.

He left the university the following May before turning eighteen to enlist in the U.S. Navy at Portland, Maine, in 1943. He served aboard the USS *Straub*, DE 181, for twenty-eight months in the Atlantic and European theaters during World War II.

He returned to the University of Maine in 1946 and graduated with a bachelor of arts degree in public management in 1949. While in college, he met Shirley Ann Smith of Hampden Highlands, Maine, and they married in 1950. They have four children.

Ron was employed respectively as town manager of Madawaska, city manager of Brewer, administrative assistant to the mayor of Westbrook, city manager of South Portland, and city administrator of Saco, all in Maine.

Ron and Shirley Stewart in Acadia National Park, 1992..

During his employment as city manager of Brewer, Ron was one of three recipients of the Maine Chamber of Commerce Award for Outstanding Young Man in Maine.

He also has been employed as sales manager of Coles Express Company in Bangor, Maine, and divisional sales manager of Hemingway Transport in Portland, Maine.

In 1974, Ron achieved a master's degree in political science from the University of Maine in Augusta.

Following retirement from public life, he was active in the community and became a selectman in the town of Wilton, Maine. He then served as Maine state president of the American Association of Retired Persons. Later, he was appointed by Governor Angus King to Maine's Long-Term Care Steering Committee. He is the public member on the State's Podiatry Medicine Licensing Board. Ron is also a volunteer with the Maine

Ombudsman Program. He visits nursing homes in Freeport weekly to check on the quality of care, and enjoys chatting with the residents.

He and Shirley now live in Bath, Maine.